rororo sprachen
Herausgegeben von
Ludwig Moos

Unsere häufigsten Fehler im Englischen sind typisch deutsch. Das gilt besonders für den Gebrauch der Zeiten, deren Ähnlichkeit zu tückischen Verwechslungen führt. Und Zeiten braucht man in jedem Satz. «Better Times» benutzt wie das erfolgreiche «Speak you English?» ein im Unterricht erprobtes Übungsprogramm, das auf dem Prinzip von Test, Kontrolle und Wiederholung beruht. Gezielt, doch ohne ödes Pauken werden so die Zeit-Fehler verlernt, die selbst der sprachgeübte Schüler, Tourist oder Geschäftsmann immer wieder macht.

Gunther Bischoff, Leiter der American School in Hamburg, hat auch ein Programm zum Verlernen typisch deutscher Englischfehler entwickelt: «Speak you English?» (rororo sprachen 6857). Außerdem liegt von ihm vor: «Managing Manager English» (rororo sprachen 7129).

TENSES

Gunther Bischoff

Better Times

Ein leichtes Programm zum richtigen Gebrauch der englischen Zeiten

rororo

Rowohlt

Dedicated to Mr. Gary McManama, without whom this book would never have been written.

46.–48. Tausend September 1999

Originalausgabe
Veröffentlicht im Rowohlt Taschenbuch Verlag GmbH, Reinbek bei Hamburg, Mai 1986

Redaktion Ludwig Moos
Umschlagentwurf Gerd Huss / Peter Wippermann
Satz Helvetica (Linotron 202)
Gesamtherstellung Clausen & Bosse, Leck
Printed in Germany
ISBN 3 499 17987 3

Einführung

Sie sprechen Englisch. Mit einer Reihe typisch deutscher Fehler im Englischen haben Sie keine Probleme mehr, da Sie mein erstes Buch «Speak you English?» bereits erfolgreich durchgearbeitet haben. Eines stört Sie allerdings noch: Ihre Unsicherheit im Gebrauch der berüchtigten englischen Zeiten.

Die englischen Zeiten sind nicht nur darum gefährliche Klippen, weil einige von ihnen Differenzierungen erlauben, die im Deutschen nicht möglich sind, sondern auch weil sie deutschen Zeiten teuflisch ähnlich klingen, mit denen sie nichts gemeinsam haben. Und da Zeiten in jedem Satz vorkommen, ist die Gefahr, sich unrichtig auszudrücken, ständig präsent.

Sie haben nun die Möglichkeit, mit Zeitfehlern gründlich aufzuräumen. Mit diesem Buch können Sie sich die häufigsten Fehler, die Deutsche im Umgang mit den wichtigsten englischen Zeiten machen, nach der gleichen Methode wie bei «Speak you English?» abüben – der Methode, Englisch durch Englisch zu lernen. Sie wird zur «Nachbehandlung» eingesetzt, der sich alle, die Grundkenntnisse in der englischen Sprache haben, unterziehen können, die aber auch für Fortgeschrittene erfahrungsgemäß angebracht ist.

Der Aufbau des Lernprogramms beruht auf dem Prinzip von Test und Kontrolle. Beim Durcharbeiten ist zu beachten:

- Auf jeweils einer rechten Seite stehen richtige und fehlerhafte Sätze unterschiedslos nebeneinander (Übungen). Versuchen Sie rasch anzugeben, wo welcher Fehler steckt.
- Nach dem Umblättern können Sie prüfen, ob Sie richtig verbessert oder Fehler übersehen haben (Lösungen). Sie finden alle Übungssätze der vorherigen Seite wiederholt, wobei Fehlerkorrekturen halbfett hervorgehoben sind und Ziffern auf die grammatikalischen Erläuterungen im Anhang verweisen.
- Jeder fehlerhafte Satz enthält nur einen Fehler. Jeder Fehler wird zunächst in dichter Abfolge wiederholt und dann mit größerem Abstand – zur «Schlußkontrolle» des Übungserfolgs – noch einmal gebracht.
- Jeder Fehler wird so oft wiederholt, daß Sie ihn gründlich verlernen können. Die Wiederholungshäufigkeit stützt sich auf praktische Unterrichtserfahrungen.
- Je schneller Sie die Übungen durcharbeiten, desto wirksamer werden Sie Ihre Fehler los.

Ian Bacon, David Duke, Maria Galffy und Jodi Proto danke ich für das englische Korrekturlesen.

Gunther Bischoff

Übungen und Lösungen

Übung 1

1. I drive my car to work every morning.
2. Today, Mrs. Brown is wearing her best dress.
3. The teacher now opens the window.
4. The pupil is always doing his homework in the afternoon.
5. The author now writes his third novel this year.
6. We usually go to New York by plane.
7. She is never coming to work on time.
8. At present, she is learning to play the violin.
9. The sun always rises in the East.
10. We look for our lost parrot. Can you help us?
11. The airplane is taking off at the same time every day.
12. The pop group is now singing its latest hit.
13. It is often raining in Hamburg in autumn.
14. The telephone is ringing. Please answer it.
15. I freeze! The temperature in this room is only 60 degrees!

Lösung 1

1. I drive my car to work every morning.
2. Today, Mrs. Brown is wearing her best dress.
3. The teacher **is** now **opening** the window. **1**
4. The pupil always **does** his homework in the afternoon. **2**
5. The author **is** now **writing** his third novel this year. **1**
6. We usually go to New York by plane.
7. She never **comes** to work on time. **2**
8. At present, she is learning to play the violin.
9. The sun always rises in the East.
10. We **are looking** for our lost parrot. Can you help us? **1**
11. The airplane **takes off** at the same time every day. **2**
12. The pop group is now singing its latest hit.
13. It often **rains** in Hamburg in autumn. **2**
14. The telephone is ringing. Please answer it.
15. I **am freezing**! The temperature in this room is only 60 degrees! **1**

Übung 2

1. It is snowing very hard now.
2. The young man is standing on the corner at the moment.
3. He is giving me the same thing for my birthday every year.
4. Sometimes, we get up early, but on weekends we sleep longer.
5. I now read a very interesting book.
6. The girl is always eating corn flakes for breakfast.
7. Our dog chases cats every day.
8. At the moment, we sit on our chairs.
9. I drink a cup of tea now.
10. We are always watching the news on television.
11. Mrs. Johnson sits in front of Mr. Black at the moment.
12. Our teacher always writes the exercises on the board.
13. Mr. Jones is leaving his office right now.
14. Mr. Smith works in his office from Monday till Friday.
15. She is smoking too many cigarettes every day.

Lösung 2

1. It is snowing very hard now.
2. The young man is standing on the corner at the moment.
3. He **gives** me the same thing for my birthday every year. **2**
4. Sometimes, we get up early, but on weekends we sleep longer.
5. I **am** now **reading** a very interesting book. **1**
6. The girl always **eats** corn flakes for breakfast. **2**
7. Our dog chases cats every day.
8. At the moment, we **are sitting** on our chairs. **1**
9. I **am drinking** a cup of tea now. **1**
10. We always **watch** the news on television. **2**
11. Mrs. Johnson **is sitting** in front of Mr. Black at the moment. **1**
12. Our teacher always writes the exercises on the board.
13. Mr. Jones is leaving his office right now.
14. Mr. Smith works in his office from Monday till Friday.
15. She **smokes** too many cigarettes every day. **2**

Übung 3

1. Are you taking a break right now?
2. Does he write a letter to his girlfriend now?
3. Does she normally visit her aunt on Sundays?
4. Listen! The doorbell rings.
5. Isn't he ever enjoying popular music?
6. The Smiths don't want to take a vacation this year.
7. We don't listen to the radio at the moment – we watch TV.
8. We aren't usually buying our clothes in that store.
9. Her jacket is presently hanging on the hanger.
10. Mrs. Jackson sits at the hairdresser's at the moment.
11. Are you always drinking too much at parties?
12. John is currently working on a new project for his boss.
13. Are you always making so many mistakes in your work?
14. Look! The sun is shining.
15. Do you begin work at the same time every morning?

Lösung 3

1. Are you taking a break right now?
2. **Is** he **writing** a letter to his girlfriend now? **1**
3. Does she normally visit her aunt on Sundays?
4. Listen! The doorbell **is ringing**. **1**
5. **Doesn't** he ever **enjoy** popular music? **2**
6. The Smiths don't want to take a vacation this year.
7. We **are** not **listening** to the radio at the moment – we **are watching** TV. **1**
8. We **don't** usually **buy** our clothes in that store. **2**
9. Her jacket is presently hanging on the hanger.
10. Mrs. Jackson **is sitting** at the hairdresser's at the moment. **1**
11. **Do** you always **drink** too much at parties? **2**
12. John is currently working on a new project for his boss.
13. **Do** you always **make** so many mistakes in your work? **2**
14. Look! The sun is shining.
15. Do you begin work at the same time every morning?

Übung 4

1. Are you always eating the same thing for breakfast?
2. The mother is now telling her children a bedtime story.
3. You don't normally take this train to work, do you?
4. A strong wind is currently blowing from the West.
5. We are spending our vacation in the United States every year.
6. I'm carrying an umbrella every time it rains.
7. Do you now prepare for your trip to China?
8. At the moment, the father is spanking his son and the mother is scolding her daughter.
9. They play the national anthem on television. Can you hear it?
10. Does she usually take an afternoon nap?
11. The Smiths are currently sailing to New York aboard the Queen Elizabeth II.
12. Is he ever washing his car in winter?
13. He never remembers his wife's birthday.
14. Please be quiet. The baby sleeps.
15. We often hike in the mountains in summer.

Lösung 4

1. **Do** you always **eat** the same thing for breakfast? **2**
2. The mother is now telling her children a bedtime story.
3. You don't normally take this train to work, do you?
4. A strong wind is currently blowing from the West.
5. We **spend** our vacation in the United States every year. **2**
6. I **carry** an umbrella every time it rains. **2**
7. **Are** you now **preparing** for your trip to China? **1**
8. At the moment, the father is spanking his son and the mother is scolding her daughter.
9. They **are playing** the national anthem on television. Can you hear it? **1**
10. Does she usually take an afternoon nap?
11. The Smiths are currently sailing to New York aboard the Queen Elizabeth II.
12. **Does** he ever **wash** his car in winter? **2**
13. He never remembers his wife's birthday.
14. Please be quiet. The baby **is sleeping.** **1**
15. We often hike in the mountains in summer.

Übung 5

1. We will go to France next week.
2. They often write letters to their friends.
3. She is in Leeds General Hospital tomorrow.
4. He will complete his training period in August.
5. She visits her grandmother at the moment.
6. Don't you ever get tired of hamburgers?
7. What do you currently think about?
8. We buy a new car next year.
9. Are you often falling asleep in front of the television?
10. Mr. Smith's son will soon begin school.
11. At what time are you getting up on Sundays?
12. The woman has a baby next month.
13. Please don't disturb us. We are trying to find an answer to all our problems.
14. Jane will speak to her friend about it tomorrow morning.
15. In my next life, I come back to earth as a frog.

Lösung 5

1. We will go to France next week.
2. They often write letters to their friends.
3. She **will be (is going to be)** in Leeds General Hospital tomorrow. **3**
4. He will complete his training period in August. **3**
5. She **is visiting** her grandmother at the moment. **1**
6. Don't you ever get tired of hamburgers?
7. What **are** you currently **thinking** about? **1**
8. We **will buy (are buying, are going to buy)** a new car next year. **3**
9. **Do** you often **fall** asleep in front of the television? **2**
10. Mr. Smith's son will soon begin school.
11. At what time **do** you **get** up on Sundays? **2**
12. The woman **will have (is having, is going to have)** a baby next month. **3**
13. Please don't disturb us. We are trying to find an answer to all our problems.
14. Jane will speak to her friend about it tomorrow morning.
15. In my next life, I **will come (am coming, am going to come)** back to earth as a frog. **3**

Übung 6

1. Will you travel to New York next year?
2. He's often looking for his lost keys.
3. We don't normally drink champagne for breakfast.
4. She notices her mistake tomorrow, but then it's too late.
5. At the moment, our cat is chasing the neighbor's parakeet.
6. Are you always enjoying eating out in restaurants?
7. He is going to buy his wife a mink coat for Christmas.
8. Don't interrupt Mr. Smith. He prepares his speech now.
9. When day will you return from your business trip?
10. Oh, look! It's raining. But you carry an umbrella.
11. When are you going to install a new bathroom in your house?
12. We never go to bed later than midnight.
13. Why do you going to paint your house pink?
14. Do you ski on your next vacation?
15. Please turn off the radio. It's still on.

Lösung 6

1. Will you travel to New York next year?

2. He often **looks** for his lost keys. **2**

3. We don't normally drink champagne for breakfast.

4. She **will notice (is going to notice)** her mistake tomorrow, but then it **will be (is going to be)** too late. **3**

5. At the moment, our cat is chasing the neighbor's parakeet.

6. **Do** you always **enjoy** eating out in restaurants? **2**

7. He is going to buy his wife a mink coat for Christmas.

8. Don't interrupt Mr. Smith. He **is preparing** his speech now. **1**

9. When will you return from your business trip?

10. Oh, look! It's raining. But you **are carrying** an umbrella. **1**

11. When are you going to install a new bathroom in your house?

12. We never go to bed later than midnight.

13. Why **are** you **going to paint (will you paint)** your house pink? **3**

14. **Will** you **ski (are** you **skiing, are** you **going to ski)** on your next vacation? **3**

15. Please turn off the radio. It's still running.

Übung 7

1. They are now drilling for oil in my back yard.
2. Are you going to look for a new suit on Saturday?
3. Mrs. Jones is going to church on Sundays.
4. Do you buy eggs at the market tomorrow?
5. You're never listening to what I'm saying.
6. You don't ever get tired of working, do you?
7. They are building a new house soon.
8. It's 10 a. m.! When are you going to get up?
9. Do you currently making plans for a cruise in the Mediterranean?
10. He comes to the party tomorrow.
11. The barber cuts my hair every week.
12. When will you finish your report?
13. John is opening the door right now, and the burglar is waiting behind it.
14. I am sure we enjoy ourselves very much at the movies tomorrow evening.
15. We will take a break for lunch in half an hour.

Lösung 7

1. They are now drilling for oil in my back yard.

2. Are you going to look for a new suit on Saturday?

3. Mrs. Jones **goes** to church on Sundays. **2**

4. **Will** you **buy** (**are** you **buying, are** you **going to buy**) eggs at the market tomorrow? **3**

5. You never **listen** to what I **say**. **2**

6. You don't ever get tired of working, do you?

7. They are building a new house soon.

8. It's 10 a. m.! When are you going to get up?

9. **Are** you currently **making** plans for a cruise in the Mediterranean? **1**

10. He **will come (is coming, is going to come)** to the party tomorrow. **3**

11. The barber cuts my hair every week.

12. When will you finish your report?

13. John is opening the door right now, and the burglar is waiting behind it.

14. I am sure we **will enjoy (are going to enjoy)** ourselves very much at the movies tomorrow evening. **3**

15. We will take a break for lunch in half an hour.

Übung 8

1. The dress designer now shows his latest models at the fashion fair.
2. I'm not normally smoking such strong cigars.
3. We all go to the zoo next week and visit the monkeys.
4. You will meet your girlfriend at the station, won't you?
5. You know you can't always have your own way, don't you?
6. The woman is currently swimming the English Channel for the fifth time.
7. We are taking the first plane to Los Angeles.
8. At what time will you meet Mrs. Smith for lunch?
9. Look in the sky! The sky-diver hangs from his parachute.
10. He writes a letter of complaint to the company next week.
11. What do you think about Sophia Loren?
12. The young man is learning three foreign languages at the same time.
13. She won't play golf next week; she'll do it this afternoon.
14. Are you always taking orders from your boss?
15. Do you grow carrots in your garden next summer?

Lösung 8

1. The dress designer **is** now **showing** his latest models at the fashion fair. **1**

2. I **do** not normally **smoke** such strong cigars. **2**

3. We **will** all **go (are** all **going, are** all **going to go)** to the zoo next week and **will visit (are visiting, are going to visit)** the monkeys. **3**

4. You will meet your girlfriend at the station, won't you?

5. You know you can't always have your own way, don't you?

6. The woman is currently swimming the English Channel for the fifth time.

7. We are taking the first plane to Los Angeles.

8. At what time will you meet Mrs. Smith for lunch?

9. Look in the sky! The sky-diver **is hanging** from his parachute. **1**

10. He **will write (is writing, is going to write)** a letter of complaint to the company next week. **3**

11. What do you think about Sophia Loren?

12. The young man is learning three foreign languages at the same time.

13. She won't play golf next week; she'll do it this afternoon.

14. **Do** you always **take** orders from your boss? **2**

15. **Will** you **grow (are** you **growing, are** you **going to grow)** carrots in your garden next summer? **3**

Übung 9

1. The maid sets the table later for our dinner party.

2. Look! The tightrope-walker walks from one skyscraper to another!

3. Do you keep your neighbor's cat for her next week?

4. Will the sun shine tomorrow?

5. When we're going on vacation, we're always taking our grandmother with us.

6. We seldom fly to Spain because it's so expensive.

7. I attend the concert at my son's school next Friday.

8. Oh, be careful! You're tearing your coat on that nail!

9. When do you choose a name for your baby daughter?

10. You're never telling jokes, are you?

11. Will you let your son go to the picnic next Sunday?

12. The singer is soon going to sing a solo at Carnegie Hall.

13. Do you pay your bill for the car repair soon?

14. We frequently buy ice-cream at that stand.

15. Where are you staying in Berlin next week?

Lösung 9

1. The maid **will set (is setting, is going to set)** the table later for our dinner party. **3**

2. Look! The tightrope-walker **is walking** from one skyscraper to another! **1**

3. **Will** you **keep, (are** you **keeping, are** you **going to keep)** your neighbor's cat for her next week? **3**

4. Will the sun shine tomorrow?

5. When we **go** on vacation, we always **take** our grandmother with us. **2**

6. We seldom fly to Spain because it's so expensive.

7. I **will attend (am attending, am going to attend)** the concert at my son's school next Friday. **3**

8. Oh, be careful! You're tearing your coat on that nail!

9. When **will** you **choose (are** you **choosing, are** you **going to choose)** a name for your baby daughter? **3**

10. You never **tell** jokes, do you? **2**

11. Will you let your son go to the picnic next Sunday?

12. The singer is soon going to sing a solo at Carnegie Hall.

13. **Will** you **pay (are** you **paying, are** you **going to pay)** your bill for the car repair soon? **3**

14. We frequently buy ice-cream at that stand.

15. Where are you staying in Berlin next week?

Übung 10

1. Last week, we visited our friends in France.
2. Next week, they visit us.
3. She drank a cup of coffee for breakfast yesterday morning.
4. We are currently spending too much money on clothing.
5. They have an accident on their way to work yesterday.
6. What are you giving your father for Christmas next year?
7. He's in court last month.
8. Does she always wear a knitted dress on such hot days?
9. I'm going out to lunch now. Do you join me?
10. The trainer presently shows the athlete how to run faster.
11. We move to Hamburg six years ago.
12. How many hours are you sleeping every night?
13. Is your favorite team winning the football game at present?
14. We saw a good movie on television last night.
15. Do you come to visit me next month?

Lösung 10

1. Last week, we visited our friends in France.
2. Next week, they **will visit (are visiting, are going to visit)** us. **3**
3. She drank a cup of coffee for breakfast yesterday morning.
4. We are currently spending too much money on clothing.
5. They **had** an accident on their way to work yesterday. **4**
6. What are you giving your father for Christmas next year?
7. He **was** in court last month. **4**
8. Does she always wear a knitted dress on such hot days?
9. I'm going out to lunch now. **Will** you **join (are** you **joining, are** you **going to join)** me? **3**
10. The trainer **is** presently **showing** the athlete how to run faster. **1**
11. We **moved** to Hamburg six years ago. **4**
12. How many hours **do** you **sleep** every night? **2**
13. Is your favorite team winning the football game at present?
14. We saw a good movie on television last night.
15. **Will** you **come (are** you **coming, are** you **going to come)** to visit me next month? **3**

Übung 11

1. The saleswoman became ill at work yesterday.
2. You're shutting that window before leaving, aren't you?
3. The Millers are in London last weekend.
4. The man found a fly in his soup at the restaurant yesterday.
5. He is 40 on his next birthday.
6. Did you turn off the gas before you left for work this morning?
7. They caught many fish on their last fishing trip.
8. Last Sunday, we make plans for a weekend trip.
9. It is raining now, so we can't go to the playground.
10. We are never wearing a sports jacket when we go to the opera.
11. Why did you leave the theater yesterday before the end of the performance?
12. Did you paid too much for your new shoes?
13. You weren't here when I came this morning, were you?
14. The man was late for work twelve times last month.
15. She didn't understood the instructions for baking the cake when she tried it yesterday.

Lösung 11

1. The saleswoman became ill at work yesterday.
2. You're shutting that window before leaving, aren't you?
3. The Millers **were** in London last weekend. **4**
4. The man found a fly in his soup at the restaurant yesterday.
5. He **will be (is going to be)** 40 on his next birthday. **3**
6. Did you turn off the gas before you left for work this morning?
7. They caught many fish on their last fishing trip.
8. Last Sunday, we **made** plans for a weekend trip. **4**
9. It is raining now, so we can't go to the playground.
10. We never **wear** a sports jacket when we go to the opera. **2**
11. Why did you leave the theater yesterday before the end of the performance?
12. **Did** you **pay** too much for your new shoes? **4**
13. You weren't here when I came this morning, were you?
14. The man was late for work twelve times last month.
15. She **didn't understand** the instructions for baking the cake when she tried it yesterday. **4**

Übung 12

1. Can you hear the music? The band plays our song.
2. The telephone just rang. Did anyone answer it?
3. They come to work late every day last week.
4. Don't bother him now. He's balancing a ball on his nose for his act in the circus.
5. Last autumn we stayed in a cabin in the mountains.
6. Do you got a bad cold when it rained last week?
7. What did your boss answer when you ask him for a raise?
8. We're spending next weekend at my parents' house.
9. Did you read the article in the newspaper yesterday?
10. What time do you eat breakfast every morning?
11. We must pay a traffic fine last week.
12. At the last company party, Mr. Smith drank so much that he forgot his own name.
13. They couldn't found their car.
14. Did you enjoy your first flight, or was the weather bad?
15. Do you sell your house to the first bidder or to the highest bidder when it goes on sale next week?

Lösung 12

1. Can you hear the music? The band **is playing** our song. **1**
2. The telephone just rang. Did anyone answer it?
3. They **came** to work late every day last week. **4**
4. Don't bother him now. He's balancing a ball on his nose for his act in the circus.
5. Last autumn we stayed in a cabin in the mountains.
6. **Did** you **get** a bad cold when it rained last week? **4**
7. What did your boss answer when you **asked** him for a raise? **4**
8. We're spending next weekend at my parents' house.
9. Did you read the article in the newspaper yesterday?
10. What time do you eat breakfast every morning?
11. We **had to pay** a traffic fine last week. **4**
12. At the last company party, Mr. Smith drank so much that he forgot his own name.
13. They **couldn't find** their car. **4**
14. Did you enjoy your first flight, or was the weather bad?
15. **Will** you **sell (are** you **selling, are** you **going to sell)** your house to the first bidder or to the highest bidder when it goes on sale next week? **3**

Übung 13

1. We heard the news on the radio on our way home frome the beach yesterday.
2. Do you take your radio with you when you go next week?
3. The astronauts began their journey a month ago.
4. Do you watch television this evening?
5. Must they stop playing football when it started to rain yesterday?
6. Why didn't you come when I called you earlier?
7. Will you meet your friends after work today?
8. She's never finding four-leaf clovers.
9. How did you burnt your hand?
10. He isn't normally hearing poorly, is he?
11. Hurry up! The taxi's waiting!
12. I'm taking my car with me to England next month.
13. At present, he tells me all his secrets.
14. He must cancelled a trip when his wife became ill last week.
15. You should never lend money to your best friends.

Lösung 13

1. We heard the news on the radio on our way home from the beach yesterday.

2. **Will** you **take (are** you **taking, are** you **going to take)** your radio with you when you go next week? **3**

3. The astronauts began their journey a month ago.

4. **Will** you **watch (are** you **watching, are** you **going to watch)** television this evening? **3**

5. **Did** they **have to stop** playing football when it started to rain yesterday? **4**

6. Why didn't you come when I called you earlier?

7. Will you meet your friends after work today?

8. She never **finds** four-leaf clovers. **2**

9. How **did** you **burn** your hand? **4**

10. He **doesn't** normally **hear** poorly, **does** he? **2**

11. Hurry up! The taxi's waiting!

12. I'm taking my car with me to England next month.

13. At present, he **is telling** me all his secrets. **1**

14. He **had to cancel** a trip when his wife became ill last week. **4**

15. You should never lend money to your best friends.

Übung 14

1. It is never snowing in July, but it is often raining.
2. I buy a lot of clothes at the end-of-season sales next week.
3. The maid is currently hanging up the laundry.
4. Ladies and gentlemen, this is the pilot. We now fly at an altitude of 10,000 meters.
5. Last week he swam in the Elbe and became ill.
6. He never wears the same suit on two consecutive days.
7. He meant to buy his daughter a birthday present the day before yesterday, but he forgot to.
8. This evening it will be cool. Then we light the fire in the fireplace.
9. Were you often freezing when you lived in Siberia?
10. I lose my pen when I visit the Grand Canyon last summer.
11. Will you be able to go skiing next winter, or won't your broken leg be healed by then?
12. Don't interrupt your father! He reads your report card.
13. Do you often sleep in the office?
14. We're going to have to spend a lot of money to get our car fixed.
15. Which book are you currently using in your French class?

Lösung 14

1. It never **snows** in July, but it often **rains**. **2**
2. I **will buy (am buying, am going to buy)** a lot of clothes at the end-of-season sales next week. **3**
3. The maid is currently hanging up the laundry.
4. Ladies and gentlemen, this is the pilot. We **are** now **flying** at an altitude of 10,000 meters. **1**
5. Last week he swam in the Elbe and became ill.
6. He never wears the same suit on two consecutive days.
7. He meant to buy his daughter a birthday present the day before yesterday, but he forgot to.
8. This evening it will be cool. Then we **will light (are lighting, are going to light)** the fire in the fireplace. **3**
9. **Did** you often **freeze** when you lived in Siberia? **4**
10. I **lost** my pen when I **visited** the Grand Canyon last summer. **4**
11. Will you be able to go skiing next winter, or won't your broken leg be healed by then?
12. Don't interrupt your father! He **is reading** your report card. **1**
13. Do you often sleep in the office?
14. We're going to have to spend a lot of money to get our car fixed.
15. Which book are you currently using in your French class?

Übung 15

1. We have lived in this apartment for ten years.
2. We have bought a new car yesterday.
3. John has worked at this firm since 1970.
4. The teacher now instructs the pupils in the use of the slide-rule.
5. The zookeeper feeds the bears at the same time every day.
6. We drive many Volkswagens since 1949.
7. Did you build a sand castle when you were at the sea yesterday?
8. The secretary types ten letters so far this morning.
9. We will miss the opening of the exhibition on Thursday because we aren't going to Hannover until Friday.
10. My grandmother has come to visit us last Friday.
11. When do you going to finally replace your old curtains?
12. I have been to London many times.
13. The fireman is frequently smoking in bed although he knows it is dangerous.
14. He is not able to work since Monday.
15. The train arrived at the station over an hour ago.

Lösung 15

1. We have lived in this apartment for ten years.
2. We **bought** a new car yesterday. **4**
3. John has worked at this firm since 1970.
4. The teacher **is** now **instructing** the pupils in the use of the slide-rule. **1**
5. The zookeeper feeds the bears at the same time every day.
6. We **have driven** many Volkswagens since 1949. **5**
7. Did you build a sand castle when you were at the sea yesterday?
8. The secretary **has typed** ten letters so far this morning. **5**
9. We will miss the opening of the exhibition on Thursday because we aren't going to Hannover until Friday.
10. My grandmother **came** to visit us last Friday. **4**
11. When **are** you **going** to finally replace your old curtains? **3**
12. I have been to London many times.
13. The fireman frequently **smokes** in bed although he knows it is dangerous. **2**
14. He **has** not **been** able to work since Monday. **5**
15. The train arrived at the station over an hour ago.

Übung 16

1. Are you ever wishing for things you can't have?
2. Have you seen the new program on television yesterday?
3. I have already shown you my passport.
4. I am stung by bees many times.
5. The father is now showing his son how to throw a football.
6. For how many years does Johnny want a pony?
7. They have already learned their lesson for today.
8. How often are you in Paris until now?
9. Have you ever eaten rattlesnake meat?
10. We leaving on the ferry tomorrow at the crack of dawn.
11. The doctor is operating on his patient six times already.
12. He runs to work a few times since March.
13. She writes all our letters for ages, doesn't she?
14. You have lost a lot of weight since Christmas.
15. You haven't forgotten our appointment for tomorrow, have you?

Lösung 16

1. **Do** you ever **wish** for things you can't have? **2**
2. **Did** you **see** the new program on television yesterday? **4**
3. I have already shown you my passport.
4. I **have been stung** by bees many times. **5**
5. The father is now showing his son how to throw a football.
6. For how many years **has** Johnny **wanted** a pony? **5**
7. They have already learned their lesson for today.
8. How often **have** you **been** in Paris until now? **5**
9. Have you ever eaten rattlesnake meat?
10. We **are leaving** on the ferry tomorrow at the crack of dawn. **3**
11. The doctor **has operated** on his patient six times already. **5**
12. He **has run** to work a few times since March. **5**
13. She **has written** all our letters for ages, **hasn't** she? **5**
14. You have lost a lot of weight since Christmas.
15. You haven't forgotten our appointment for tomorrow, have you?

Übung 17

1. Don't interrupt me; I prepare for my driving test.
2. We begin our work at 6:00 a. m. for years.
3. He has met an old friend at the airport yesterday.
4. He is in London since last Friday.
5. Did you go mountaineering last weekend?
6. For the past ten years, we buy a new car every year.
7. I have already drunk twelve cups of coffee today.
8. When do you think you arrive at the party tomorrow evening?
9. You still don't answer all of my questions.
10. His wife hasn't bought a new dress for over a month.
11. The constructor has come to look at my house last week.
12. The sick monkey hasn't eaten any bananas for three days.
13. She doesn't yet notice that her car keys are missing.
14. She's usually coming to work on time.
15. Have you ever tried «Crunchies» corn flakes?

Lösung 17

1. Don’t interrupt me; I **am preparing** for my driving test. **1**
2. We **have begun** our work at 6:00 a. m. for years. **5**
3. He **met** an old friend at the airport yesterday. **4**
4. He **has been** in London since last Friday. **5**
5. Did you go mountaineering last weekend?
6. For the past ten years, we **have bought** a new car every year. **5**
7. I have already drunk twelve cups of coffee today.
8. When do you think you **will arrive (are arriving, are going to arrive)** at the party tomorrow evening? **3**
9. You still **have** not **answered** all of my questions. **5**
10. His wife hasn’t bought a new dress for over a month.
11. The constructor **came** to look at my house last week. **4**
12. The sick monkey hasn’t eaten any bananas for three days.
13. She **hasn’t** yet **noticed** that her car keys are missing. **5**
14. She usually **comes** to work on time. **2**
15. Have you ever tried «Crunchies» corn flakes?

Übung 18

1. The angry wife still hasn't forgiven her husband for his comments.

2. Chicago is the «Windy City»; the wind is often blowing hard there.

3. The hard-working man hasn't had a vacation in many years.

4. Do you reconsider your plan yet?

5. How many years do you have a fear of bats?

6. We have thought of you many times when we were in England.

7. Have all arrangements for the state visit been made?

8. We're deciding that point tomorrow.

9. Since his arrival in Europe, he sees 14 museums and 27 churches.

10. At the moment, the two dogs fight over the bone.

11. He sails a different boat every year for six years.

12. Napoleon lost the Battle of Waterloo in 1815.

13. Does your boss already return from his dinner meeting?

14. Our chicken has already laid six eggs.

15. «John, you haven't worn this purple tie for ages.»

Lösung 18

1. The angry wife still hasn't forgiven her husband for his comments.
2. Chicago is the «Windy City»; the wind often **blows** hard there. **2**
3. The hard-working man hasn't had a vacation in many years.
4. **Have** you **reconsidered** your plan yet? **5**
5. How many years **have** you **had** a fear of bats? **5**
6. We **thought** of you many times when we were in England. **4**
7. Have all arrangements for the state visit been made?
8. We're deciding that point tomorrow.
9. Since his arrival in Europe, he **has seen** 14 museums and 27 churches. **5**
10. At the moment, the two dogs **are fighting** over the bone. **1**
11. He **has sailed** a different boat every year for six years. **5**
12. Napoleon lost the Battle of Waterloo in 1815.
13. **Has** your boss already **returned** from his dinner meeting? **5**
14. Our chicken has already laid six eggs.
15. «John, you haven't worn this purple tie for ages.»

Übung 19

1. Have you read the newspaper yet?
2. Do you practise karate for many years?
3. We have eaten in the best restaurants in the world and slept in the most expensive hotels.
4. I have told you at least a hundred times to wipe your feet before entering the house!
5. How long have you known the murderer?
6. He carries his umbrella with him every day this week.
7. She already writes at least a dozen letters this morning.
8. The band marches directly in front of us. Can you see it?
9. I have eaten cheese for breakfast every day for years.
10. Did you can see the Statue of Liberty from the plane when you flew to New York?
11. He doesn't work on his house for a long time.
12. The little girl always enjoys herself when she visits the zoo.
13. Are the defective parts already replaced?
14. He's in the conference for hours.
15. They have discussed politics on many occasions.

Lösung 19

1. Have you read the newspaper yet?

2. **Have** you **practised** karate for many years? **5**

3. We have eaten in the best restaurants in the world and slept in the most expensive hotels.

4. I have told you at least a hundred times to wipe your feet before e0001entering the house!

5. How long have you known the murderer?

6. He **has carried** his umbrella with him every day this week. **5**

7. She **has** already **written** at least a dozen letters this morning. **5**

8. The band **is marching** directly in front of us. Can you see it? **1**

9. I have eaten cheese for breakfast every day for years.

10. **Could** you **see** the Statue of Liberty from the plane when you flew to New York? **4**

11. He **hasn't worked** on his house for a long time. **5**

12. The little girl always enjoys herself when she visits the zoo.

13. **Have** the defective parts already **been replaced**? **5**

14. He **has been** in the conference for hours. **5**

15. They have discussed politics on many occasions.

Übung 20

1. Are you often listening to the news on the radio or watching it on television?

2. Have you gone to the bank yesterday?

3. His advice is helpful to us many times.

4. At present, Mr. Smith sits in his office and thinks about his speech.

5. We never wear tennis shoes to a formal dance.

6. We wanted to buy a new sofa when we were in the city, but we couldn't find the right one.

7. The movie director is currently filming in Africa.

8. Have you already taken your medicine today?

9. We are washing our car tomorrow morning.

10. The doctor has sought the nurses' aid during the operation yesterday.

11. The lady has smoked strong cigars from time to time since she was 16.

12. How many times does he travel to Rome in the last 5 years?

13. What's happening at the theater next week?

14. The water rose last night and flooded our cellar.

15. I repair my kitchen sink tomorrow.

Lösung 20

1. **Do** you often **listen** to the news on the radio or **watch** it on television? **2**

2. **Did** you **go** to the bank yesterday? **4**

3. His advice **has been** helpful to us many times. **5**

4. At present, Mr. Smith **is sitting** in his office and **thinking** about his speech. **1**

5. We never wear tennis shoes to a formal dance.

6. We wanted to buy a new sofa when we were in the city, but we couldn't find the right one.

7. The movie director is currently filming in Africa.

8. Have you already taken your medicine today?

9. We are washing our car tomorrow morning.

10. The doctor **sought** the nurses' aid during the operation yesterday. **4**

11. The lady has smoked strong cigars from time to time since she was 16.

12. How many times **has** he **travelled** to Rome in the last 5 years? **5**

13. What's happening at the theater next week?

14. The water rose last night and flooded our cellar.

15. I **will repair (am repairing, am going to repair)** my kitchen sink tomorrow. **3**

Übung 21

1. It has been raining for three solid days!
2. I water the plants in my apartment next week.
3. I have been looking for you since noon! Where have you been?
4. He is presently trying to decide between tea and coffee.
5. Must you take your dog to the veterinarian yesterday?
6. He fishes at the lake for hours! I don't know when he'll be home.
7. During lunch, the maid burst in and said the house was on fire.
8. I eat at Chinese restaurants a number of times.
9. You aren't normally wearing snow boots in summer, are you?
10. We wait for a telephone call.
11. My mother-in-law visits us ever since Christmas.
12. When we went to the birthday party, we met many old friends.
13. How many years are you married?
14. Are you going to go to the doctor this afternoon or tomorrow morning?
15. I'm not able to stop to rest when I cut the grass yesterday.

Lösung 21

1. It has been raining for three solid days!
2. I **will water (am watering, am going to water)** the plants in my apartment next week. **3**
3. I have been looking for you since noon! Where have you been?
4. He is presently trying to decide between tea and coffee.
5. **Did** you **have to take** your dog to the veterinarian yesterday? **4**
6. He **has been fishing** at the lake for hours! I don't know when he'll be home. **6**
7. During lunch, the maid burst in and said the house was on fire.
8. I **have eaten** at Chinese restaurants a number of times. **5**
9. You **don't** normally **wear** snow boots in summer, **do** you? **2**
10. We **are waiting** for a telephone call. **1**
11. My mother-in-law **has been visiting** us ever since Christmas. **6**
12. When we went to the birthday party, we met many old friends.
13. How many years **have** you **been** married? **5**
14. Are you going to go to the doctor this afternoon or tomorrow morning?
15. I **was** not **able** to stop to rest when I cut the grass yesterday. **4**

Übung 22

1. The pupil has been working on the assignment for eight hours without a break.
2. They already show that film on television so many times.
3. The baby cries. I think it's hungry.
4. The gardener pulls weeds in the garden since early this morning.
5. When we went to Denmark last week, we took the ferry.
6. The student studies at the university for the last 23 semesters.
7. How long has the artist been turning out masterpieces?
8. The teenager has been cleaning her room for the last three days.
9. Does your father send you any money in the last two years?
10. Are you always drinking a martini just before dinner?
11. We have been tricked again yesterday by a door-to-door salesman.
12. The body lies unnoticed for the last several hours.
13. He's been looking for a new job since the first of the month.
14. The expectant father paces the floor since midnight.
15. I don't ever drink vodka on an empty stomach again!

Lösung 22

1. The pupil has been working on the assignment for eight hours without a break.
2. They **have** already **shown** that film on television so many times. **5**
3. The baby **is crying**. I think it's hungry. **1**
4. The gardener **has been pulling** weeds in the garden since early this morning. **6**
5. When we went to Denmark last week, we took the ferry.
6. The student **has been studying** at the university for the last 23 semesters. **6**
7. How long has the artist been turning out masterpieces?
8. The teenager has been cleaning her room for the last three days.
9. **Has** your father **sent** you any money in the last two years? **5**
10. **Do** you always **drink** a martini just before dinner? **2**
11. We **were tricked** again yesterday by a door-to-door salesman. **4**
12. The body **has lain** unnoticed for the last several hours. **5**
13. He's been looking for a new job since the first of the month.
14. The expectant father **has been pacing** the floor since midnight. **6**
15. I **won't** ever **drink (am** not **drinking, am** not **going to drink)** vodka on an empty stomach again! **3**

Übung 23

1. She's frequently buying gasoline because her car uses so much.
2. The telephone rings constantly for days.
3. Did you ever see the Washington Monument?
4. I have taken the train to work on Monday.
5. We're going shopping for a new car next week.
6. I've been waiting for a taxi for 20 minutes.
7. Oh, your favorite song is on the radio. Do you listen?
8. She gets ready to go to the dance since five o'clock.
9. «John, you've been reading that newspaper for nearly half an hour.»
10. Because she had to wait at her dentist's office, she read an interesting article in a magazine.
11. The Dukes are in Spain since Easter.
12. He's been going to the movies every Saturday for years.
13. You've been watching television too long. Please turn it off.
14. I do my morning exercises every morning since January.
15. I write a novel for at least a year.

Lösung 23

1. She frequently **buys** gasoline because her car uses so much. **2**
2. The telephone **has been ringing** constantly for days. **6**
3. **Have** you ever **seen** the Washington Monument? **5**
4. I **took** the train to work on Monday. **4**
5. We're going shopping for a new car next week.
6. I've been waiting for a taxi for 20 minutes.
7. Oh, your favorite song is on the radio. **Are** you **listening**? **1**
8. She **has been getting** ready to go to the dance since five o'clock. **6**
9. «John, you've been reading that newspaper for nearly half an hour.»
10. Because she had to wait at her dentist's office, she read an interesting article in a magazine.
11. The Dukes **have been** in Spain since Easter. **5**
12. He's been going to the movies every Saturday for years.
13. You've been watching television too long. Please turn it off.
14. I **have been doing** my morning exercises every morning since January. **6**
15. I **have been writing** a novel for at least a year. **6**

Übung 24

1. The professor lectures for almost two hours; he began at 2:00 p. m.
2. How long have you been planning to rob a bank?
3. I see the famous singer many times; she's my neighbor.
4. Jack has been going out with Jill for nearly two years.
5. The trumpet player downstairs plays for the last half-hour.
6. Did you have to buy a new tire for your car before the inspection last week?
7. They have been taking French lessons every week since their trip to France.
8. They normally play table-tennis on Fridays.
9. They quarrel with each other ever since their wedding day.
10. They travel to the Bahamas at Christmas every year since 1965.
11. Do you think it rains on the weekend?
12. The Fire Department has been called out a number of times this month.
13. We haven't met you at the fair yesterday. Where have you been?
14. I switched on the light an hour ago and it still burns.
15. The poor woman's husband has been snoring loudly since 1:00 a. m.

Lösung 24

1. The professor **has been lecturing** for almost two hours; he began at 2:00 p. m. **6**

2. How long have you been planning to rob a bank?

3. I **have seen** the famous singer many times; she's my neighbor. **5**

4. Jack has been going out with Jill for nearly two years.

5. The trumpet player downstairs **has been playing** for the last half-hour. **6**

6. Did you have to buy a new tire for your car before the inspection last week?

7. They have been taking French lessons every week since their trip to France.

8. They normally play table-tennis on Fridays.

9. They **have been quarrelling** with each other ever since their wedding day. **6**

10. They **have been travelling** to the Bahamas at Christmas every year since 1965. **5**

11. Do you think it **will rain (is going to rain)** on the weekend? **3**

12. The Fire Department has been called out a number of times this month.

13. We **didn't meet** you at the fair yesterday. Where **were** you? **4**

14. I switched on the light an hour ago and it **is** still **burning**. **1**

15. The poor woman's husband has been snoring loudly since 1:00 a. m.

Übung 25

1. Mrs. Black has been chatting with her neighbor ever since nine o'clock this morning.
2. The baby has been crying for the past 20 minutes.
3. The carpenter makes twelve tables so far this month.
4. Mr. Jones lies in Leeds General Hospital with a broken leg ever since the accident.
5. Have you ever been atop the Empire State Building?
6. Next year, we celebrate New Year's Eve with a big party.
7. The dictator has been ruling his country for over 25 years.
8. The Smiths are travelling to China twice a year.
9. I'm so tired. I think we drive for ages.
10. The giant manufacturing company burns out of control for more than 24 hours. The firemen are still fighting the fire.
11. We have worked hard yesterday, so today we can rest.
12. The workers pour cement at the building site for hours. When will they stop?
13. I'm looking for a novel by my favorite author to give to my aunt.
14. Our postman has been delivering our post every day since 1960.
15. How long do you get up at five o'clock in the morning?

Lösung 25

1. Mrs. Black has been chatting with her neighbor ever since nine o'clock this morning.

2. The baby has been crying for the past 20 minutes.

3. The carpenter **has made** twelve tables so far this month. **5**

4. Mr. Jones **has been lying** in Leeds General Hospital with a broken leg ever since the accident. **6**

5. Have you ever been atop the Empire State Building?

6. Next year we **will celebrate (are celebrating, are going to celebrate)** New Year's Eve with a big party. **3**

7. The dictator has been ruling his country for over 25 years.

8. The Smiths **travel to** China twice a year. **2**

9. I'm so tired. I think we **have been driving** for ages. **6**

10. The giant manufacturing company **has been burning** out of control for more than 24 hours. The firemen are still fighting the fire. **6**

11. We **worked** hard yesterday, so today we can rest. **4**

12. The workers **have been pouring** cement at the building site for hours. When will they stop? **6**

13. I'm looking for a novel by my favorite author to give to my aunt.

14. Our postman has been delivering our post every day since 1960.

15. How long **have** you **been getting up** at five o'clock in the morning? **6**

Übung 26

1. How many times have you tried to telephone your friend this morning?
2. When have you heard the story about the escaped bear?
3. The housewife has been ironing for almost two hours.
4. Tomorrow, we're attending the premiere of Wagner's opera in Bayreuth.
5. The actress presently plays Lady Macbeth.
6. Do you frequently have to make excuses for your child's behavior?
7. You're sunburnt. Since when do you lie in the sun?
8. How long has the salesman been selling used cars?
9. Last month, we paid our electric bill on time.
10. Our police catches criminals with regularity for over fifty years.
11. Jeff is in the army. How long is he there already?
12. We are considering building an addition to our house at the moment.
13. Joe has been trying to light the fire in the fireplace without success for half an hour.
14. Next week, we certainly lose the match against our rivals.
15. The Queen has shaken hands with one hundred visitors yesterday.

Lösung 26

1. How many times have you tried to telephone your friend this morning?

2. When **did** you **hear** the story about the escaped bear? **4**

3. The housewife has been ironing for almost two hours.

4. Tomorrow, we're attending the premiere of Wagner's opera in Bayreuth.

5. The actress **is** presently **playing** Lady Macbeth. **1**

6. Do you frequently have to make excuses for your child's behavior?

7. You're sunburnt. Since when **have** you **been lying** in the sun? **6**

8. How long has the salesman been selling used cars?

9. Last month, we paid our electric bill on time.

10. Our police **has been catching** criminals with regularity for over fifty years. **6**

11. Jeff is in the army. How long **has** he **been** there already? **5**

12. We are considering building an addition to our house at the moment.

13. Joe has been trying to light the fire in the fireplace without success for half an hour.

14. Next week, we **will** certainly **lose (are** certainly **losing**, **are** certainly **going to lose)** the match against our rivals. **3**

15. The Queen **shook** hands with one hundred visitors yesterday. **4**

Übung 27

1. While John was washing the car, it began to rain.
2. They have finished the construction of the new airport.
3. At what age have you learned to tie your own shoes?
4. When the telephone rang, we were watching television.
5. You don't call me since last Friday. Aren't you well?
6. They have been intending to marry for ten years, but still haven't done it.
7. We discuss «Roots» at the next meeting of our literary club.
8. How long do you feel so tired? Since your illness?
9. While we drove to Holland, our car had a flat tire.
10. I see they are currently showing your old films at the film festival.
11. When are you getting your hair cut?
12. She met her neighbor while she shopped.
13. The hostess greeted us at the door when we arrived at the party yesterday afternoon.
14. I mean to write to you ever since you moved away.
15. We are frequently spending the summer weekends at the sea.

Lösung 27

1. While John was washing the car, it began to rain.

2. They have finished the construction of the new airport.

3. At what age **did** you **learn** to tie your own shoes? **4**

4. When the telephone rang, we were watching television.

5. You **haven't called** me since last Friday. **Haven't** you **been** well? **5**

6. They have been intending to marry for ten years, but still haven't done it.

7. We **will discuss (are discussing, are going to discuss)** «Roots» at the next meeting of our literary club. **3**

8. How long **have** you **been feeling** so tired? Since your illness? **6**

9. While we **were driving** to Holland, our car had a flat tire. **7**

10. I see they are currently showing your old films at the film festival.

11. When are you getting your hair cut?

12. She met her neighbor while she **was shopping**. **7**

13. The hostess greeted us at the door when we arrived at the party yesterday afternoon.

14. I **have been meaning** to write to you ever since you moved away. **6**

15. We frequently **spend** the summer weekends at the sea. **2**

Übung 28

1. The actress is buying an expensive new dress every week.
2. She walked the dog when it saw the cat and started to chase it.
3. We wanted to go to the museum yesterday, but we can't, because it was closed.
4. What were you saying when I interrupted you?
5. We have our refrigerator for almost twenty years; I think it's time to buy a new one.
6. The fuse blew just as they showed the most exciting part of the film.
7. How many years have you been giving blood at the Red Cross?
8. Do you ever fly again since the plane crash?
9. All the time the neighbor was playing his drums, I was trying to watch television.
10. I just wrote an important letter when my pen ran out of ink.
11. While we looked at old photographs, mother knitted a sweater.
12. Many pupils were standing on their chairs when the teacher entered the room.
13. The boss constantly checks his secretary's work.
14. We sat in the living room when the fire broke out.
15. At this time last year, we were living in Munich.

Lösung 28

1. The actress **buys** an expensive new dress every week. **2**
2. She **was walking** the dog when it saw the cat and started to chase it. **7**
3. We wanted to go to the museum yesterday, but we **couldn't**, because it was closed. **4**
4. What were you saying when I interrupted you?
5. We **have had** our refrigerator for almost twenty years; I think it's time to buy a new one. **5**
6. The fuse blew just as they **were showing** the most exciting part of the film. **7**
7. How many years have you been giving blood at the Red Cross?
8. **Have** you ever **flown** again since the plane crash? **5**
9. All the time the neighbor was playing his drums, I was trying to watch television.
10. I **was** just **writing** an important letter when my pen ran out of ink. **7**
11. While we **were looking** at old photographs, mother **was knitting** a sweater. **7**
12. Many pupils were standing on their chairs when the teacher entered the room.
13. The boss constantly checks his secretary's work.
14. We **were sitting** in the living room when the fire broke out. **7**
15. At this time last year, we were living in Munich.

Übung 29

1. I couldn't speak to him on the phone because he was taking a shower.

2. Last week, we have gone to the doctor's, the dentist's, and the optometrist's.

3. The roads were so crowded because so many people were returning from vacation.

4. Did you ever try to touch the tips of your toes with your fingers?

5. I got my polio vaccination last week; when are you getting yours?

6. We hunt mushrooms all morning and still don't find any.

7. Our dog now eats his meal.

8. The birds sang beautifully when I got up this morning.

9. Have you ever thought about the future?

10. The robber broke into the store when he was discovered by the night watchman.

11. What did you do at this time last year?

12. Just as she was taking down the last piece of laundry, it started to rain.

13. The doctor is checking the old man's heart every three months.

14. She tripped and fell while she was running downstairs.

15. The man bought a present for his daughter when his bus left.

Lösung 29

1. I couldn't speak to him on the phone because he was taking a shower.

2. Last week, we **went** to the doctor's, the dentist's, and the optometrist's. **4**

3. The roads were so crowded because so many people were returning from vacation.

4. **Have** you ever **tried** to touch the tips of your toes with your fingers? **5**

5. I got my polio vaccination last week; when are you getting yours?

6. We **have been hunting** mushrooms all morning and still **have** not **found** any. **6 + 5**

7. Our dog **is** now **eating** his meal. **1**

8. The birds **were singing** beautifully when I got up this morning. **7**

9. Have you ever thought about the future?

10. The robber **was breaking** into the store when he was discovered by the night watchman. **7**

11. What **were** you **doing** at this time last year? **7**

12. Just as she was taking down the last piece of laundry, it started to rain.

13. The doctor **checks** the old man's heart every three months. **2**

14. She tripped and fell while she was running downstairs.

15. The man **was buying** a present for his daughter when his bus left. **7**

Übung 30

1. Since when does he grow a beard?
2. She doesn't often give such expensive gifts, does she?
3. He was going to visit his aunt last weekend, but he didn't.
4. Did you drink a lot of champagne when you were in France?
5. While I looked through the mail, I noticed an urgent letter.
6. We were just sitting down to lunch when they arrived.
7. It seems like we've been waiting at this bus-stop for ages.
8. He's in the Bahamas ever since he left the country with his company's money.
9. The pop group sang its latest hit and all the girls in the audience screamed when the stage collapsed.
10. When we tried to call our friends in New York, we got a busy signal.
11. We hiked in the mountains just as the snowstorm struck.
12. Mary was cooking lunch all the time John was watering the flowers.
13. At this moment, the famous brain surgeon operates on his hundredth case.
14. We've often had to send for the doctor in the middle of the night.
15. Are you at the beach at this time next week?

Lösung 30

1. Since when **has** he **been growing** a beard? **6**

2. She doesn't often give such expensive gifts, does she?

3. He was going to visit his aunt last weekend, but he didn't.

4. Did you drink a lot of champagne when you were in France?

5. While I **was looking** through the mail, I noticed an urgent letter. **7**

6. We were just sitting down to lunch when they arrived.

7. It seems like we've been waiting at this bus-stop for ages.

8. He **has been** in the Bahamas ever since he left the country with his company's money. **5**

9. The pop group **was singing** its latest hit and all the girls in the audience **were screaming** when the stage collapsed. **7**

10. When we tried to call our friends in New York, we got a busy signal.

11. We **were hiking** in the mountains just as the snowstorm struck. **7**

12. Mary was cooking lunch all the time John was watering the flowers.

13. At this moment, the famous brain surgeon **is operating** on his hundredth case. **1**

14. We've often had to send for the doctor in the middle of the night.

15. **Will** you **be (are** you **going to be)** at the beach at this time next week? **3**

Übung 31

1. He has a backache because he's been working in the garden all day.
2. My cat presently lies in its basket and washes its face.
3. Did you do your homework all the time you were sitting in your room?
4. We received our visas while we were packing our bags for the trip to China.
5. How many bottles of beer do you drink today?
6. How long do you collect stamps already?
7. We have seen all the good art museums of Italy.
8. Show me where you were standing when the bomb exploded.
9. Did you wear your glasses when you were hit in the face by the snowball?
10. Mr. Smith was trying to listen to a sports broadcast while his wife was practising the piano.
11. John and I are visiting art museums on Sundays.
12. Representatives of the two superpowers signed a treaty when war broke out.
13. The artist sneezed just as he was finishing his painting.
14. We have seen the big battleship in the harbor last weekend.
15. We left for the dance when our friends dropped in unexpectedly.

Lösung 31

1. He has a backache because he's been working in the garden all day.

2. My cat **is** presently **lying** in its basket and **washing** its face. **1**

3. **Were** you **doing** your homework all the time you were sitting in your room? **7**

4. We received our visas while we were packing our bags for the trip to China.

5. How many bottles of beer **have** you **drunk** today? **5**

6. How long **have** you **been collecting** stamps already? **6**

7. We have seen all the good art museums of Italy.

8. Show me where you were standing when the bomb exploded.

9. **Were** you **wearing** your glasses when you were hit in the face by the snowball? **7**

10. Mr. Smith was trying to listen to a sports broadcast while his wife was practising the piano.

11. John and I **visit** art museums on Sundays. **2**

12. Representatives of the two superpowers **were signing** a treaty when war broke out. **7**

13. The artist sneezed just as he was finishing his painting.

14. We **saw** the big battleship in the harbor last weekend. **4**

15. We **were leaving** for the dance when our friends dropped in unexpectedly. **7**

Übung 32

1. The secretary is sorting the mail every morning and answering the letters every afternoon.
2. He smelled the rose when the bee stung him.
3. The police arrived as the drunken driver was trying to drive away from the accident.
4. They discuss the terms of peace ever since the end of the war.
5. While he looked for his lost key in the sofa, he found three pens, four marbles, and 27 cents in change.
6. He's going to become a father soon, and he thinks his wife is going to have triplets.
7. We lost our way while we were driving along the country roads at night.
8. On my trip to Spain last winter, I was looking at the famous old buildings.
9. Did you still sleep when I called you this morning?
10. Who's been smoking my cigarettes? They're all gone.
11. He cut himself while he shaved this morning.
12. The woman was stopped for shoplifting just as she was leaving the store.
13. The newly-married woman has telephoned her mother every single day this month.
14. My brother can speak Chinese, but at the moment he speaks English.
15. I am in Denmark many times; the last time was yesterday.

Lösung 32

1. The secretary **sorts** the mail every morning and **answers** the letters every afternoon. **2**
2. He **was smelling** the rose when the bee stung him. **7**
3. The police arrived as the drunken driver was trying to drive away from the accident.
4. They **have been discussing** the terms of peace ever since the end of the war. **6**
5. While he **was looking** for his lost key in the sofa, he found three pens, four marbles, and 27 cents in change. **7**
6. He's going to become a father soon, and he thinks his wife is going to have triplets.
7. We lost our way while we were driving along the country roads at night.
8. On my trip to Spain last winter, I **looked** at the famous old buildings. **4**
9. **Were** you still **sleeping** when I called you this morning? **7**
10. Who's been smoking my cigarettes? They're all gone.
11. He cut himself while he **was shaving** this morning. **7**
12. The woman was stopped for shoplifting just as she was leaving the store.
13. The newly-married woman has telephoned her mother every single day this month.
14. My brother can speak Chinese, but at the moment he **is speaking** English. **1**
15. I **have been** in Denmark many times; the last time was yesterday. **5**

Übung 33

1. It's been dark for nearly an hour.
2. She was closing the window when she knocked the plant off the ledge.
3. What do you wear to your tennis match tomorrow?
4. Look! That man tries to murder his wife!
5. The cat tries to catch the bird for at least an hour.
6. Don't you ever want to leave your home again?
7. We won't be able to take a hot shower in the morning because there's no water.
8. Were you pulling weeds all the time you were in the garden?
9. When we were in Switzerland, we enjoyed the scenery.
10. We are already in Vienna a number of times.
11. We are currently spending much too much on sweets.
12. Just as we were driving down the steepest part of the mountain, our brakes gave out.
13. We are never taking a trip without our cat.
14. How long have you been answering the telephone at work?
15. When have you bought your new house?

Lösung 33

1. It's been dark for nearly an hour.

2. She was closing the window when she knocked the plant off the ledge.

3. What **will** you **wear (are** you **wearing, are** you **going to wear)** to your tennis match tomorrow? **3**

4. Look! That man **is trying** to murder his wife! **1**

5. The cat **has been trying** to catch the bird for at least an hour. **6**

6. Don't you ever want to leave your home again?

7. We won't be able to take a hot shower in the morning because there's no water.

8. Were you pulling weeds all the time you were in the garden?

9. When we were in Switzerland, we enjoyed the scenery.

10. We **have** already **been** in Vienna a number of times. **5**

11. We are currently spending much too much on sweets.

12. Just as we were driving down the steepest part of the mountain our brakes gave out.

13. We never **take** a trip without our cat. **2**

14. How long have you been answering the telephone at work?

15. When **did** you **buy** your new house? **4**

Übung 34

1. After we had eaten, we took a walk around the lake.
2. At this time yesterday, we were still enjoying the mountains of Switzerland.
3. He tries to get himself elected mayor for the past fifteen years.
4. Because you are so helpful for so many years, I am leaving you a big chunk of money in my will.
5. After the dust had settled, we could see the damage from the explosion.
6. After he lit his cigarette, he burned his fingers on the match.
7. Will you please turn down your radio? The noise drives me crazy.
8. After he lost all his money at the gambling table, the man unhappily left the casino.
9. When I noticed my neighbor in the crowd, she stood near the speakers' platform.
10. The big-game hunter has shot four elephants on his last African safari.
11. He's reading four or five pages in his book every evening before he goes to sleep.
12. Our dog finally came in after he had been called at least half a dozen times.
13. After they sold their house, they moved to California.
14. Aunt Martha walked in just as we talked about her.
15. Have you known the Smiths for more than five years?

Lösung 34

1. After we had eaten, we took a walk around the lake.

2. At this time yesterday, we were still enjoying the mountains of Switzerland.

3. He **has been trying** to get himself elected mayor for the past fifteen years. **6**

4. Because you **have been** so helpful for so many years, I am leaving you a big chunk of money in my will. **5**

5. After the dust had settled, we could see the damage from the explosion.

6. After he **had lit** his cigarette, he burned his fingers on the match. **8**

7. Will you please turn down your radio? The noise **is driving** me crazy. **1**

8. After he **had lost** all his money at the gambling table, the man unhappily left the casino. **8**

9. When I noticed my neighbor in the crowd, she **was standing** near the speakers' platform. **7**

10. The big-game hunter **shot** four elephants on his last African safari. **4**

11. He **reads** four or five pages in his book every evening before he goes to sleep. **2**

12. Our dog finally came in after he had been called at least half a dozen times.

13. After they **had sold** their house, they moved to California. **8**

14. Aunt Martha walked in just as we **were talking** about her. **7**

15. Have you known the Smiths for more than five years?

Übung 35

1. After she tried on dozens of shoes, Mrs. Jackson finally bought a pair.
2. Are you able to visit your daughter since taking over your new job?
3. The man has been sitting at the bar since three o'clock this afternoon.
4. A parent is always trying to decide what is best for his children.
5. He felt ill because he had eaten too many sweets.
6. While we waited for a taxi, Mr. Walker stopped and picked us up.
7. Will you be able to drive to Munich next weekend, or will your leg still be in a cast?
8. After the postman delivered our post, he was bitten by the neighbor's dog.
9. Oh, look! The sun finally breaks through the clouds.
10. Have you been able to reach your boss to tell him about your leaving the company?
11. How long do you try to reach me so far this morning?
12. He didn't open the window because someone else had already opened it.
13. Do you know that the Bacons went to Africa last week?
14. When we reached the meeting place, our friends had already arrived.
15. We only drove twenty miles before our car ran out of gas.

Lösung 35

1. After she **had tried** on dozens of shoes, Mrs. Jackson finally bought a pair. **8**

2. **Have** you **been able** to visit your daughter since taking over your new job? **5**

3. The man has been sitting at the bar since three o'clock this afternoon.

4. A parent always **tries** to decide what is best for his children. **2**

5. He felt ill because he had eaten too many sweets.

6. While we **were waiting** for a taxi, Mr. Walker stopped and picked us up. **7**

7. Will you be able to drive to Munich next weekend, or will your leg still be in a cast?

8. After the postman **had delivered** our post, he was bitten by the neighbor's dog. **8**

9. Oh, look! The sun **is** finally **breaking** through the clouds. **1**

10. Have you been able to reach your boss to tell him about your leaving the company?

11. How long **have** you **been trying** to reach me so far this morning? **6**

12. He didn't open the window because someone else had already opened it.

13. Do you know that the Bacons went to Africa last week?

14. When we reached the meeting place, our friends had already arrived.

15. We **had** only **driven** twenty miles before our car ran out of gas. **8**

Übung 36

1. I've warned you at least a hundred times not to play with fire.
2. The passengers could get off after the train reached the station.
3. When the comet is discovered last year, it is named after its discoverer.
4. He gave up skiing because he had broken his leg so often.
5. Do you watch the quiz show on television tomorrow evening?
6. Does the child play outside in the rain since early this morning?
7. They wanted to go to the cinema, but she already saw the film.
8. Don't hang up! Aunt Mary now enters the house; you can talk to her in a minute.
9. He told the police that someone took all his money.
10. We discovered that the gas man came before we got up.
11. As soon as the rain was stopping, the soccer match was resumed.
12. Every time I sit down to dinner, the telephone is ringing.
13. He broke his tooth while he ate the stale candy.
14. The journalist reported that the accident had occurred at 6:00 p.m.
15. We were camping outside when the earthquake struck, so we were not injured.

Lösung 36

1. I've warned you at least a hundred times not to play with fire.
2. The passengers could get off after the train **had reached** the station. **8**
3. When the comet **was discovered** last year, it **was named** after its discoverer. **4**
4. He gave up skiing because he had broken his leg so often.
5. **Will** you **watch (are** you **watching, are** you **going to watch)** the quiz show on television tomorrow evening? **3**
6. **Has** the child been **playing** outside in the rain since early this morning? **6**
7. They wanted to go to the cinema, but she **had** already **seen** the film. **8**
8. Don't hang up! Aunt Mary **is** now **entering** the house; you can talk to her in a minute. **1**
9. He told the police that someone **had taken** all his money. **8**
10. We discovered that the gas man **had come** before we got up. **8**
11. As soon as the rain **had stopped**, the soccer match was resumed. **8**
12. Every time I sit down to dinner, the telephone **rings**. **2**
13. He broke his tooth while he **was eating** the stale candy. **7**
14. The journalist reported that the accident had occurred at 6:00 p.m.
15. We were camping outside when the earthquake struck, so we were not injured.

Übung 37

1. I was ill this year, but next year I work at my father's company during the school holiday.

2. The architect has been drawing the plans for the new bank since November.

3. After the rabbit had delivered all the Easter eggs, he hopped back to his hole.

4. She plays tennis many times so far this summer.

5. I had only read a few pages when I had to stop.

6. When I came home from work yesterday, I turned on the light because it is already dark.

7. The cleaning lady swept the floor after she polished the windows.

8. Call the police quickly! The man has been badly hurt in an accident.

9. Are you usually hurrying so much on your way to work?

10. Did you go anywhere after you ate out at the restaurant?

11. After we listened to his speech for nearly an hour, we left the lecture.

12. After the cow was butchered, the meat was cut, wrapped, and frozen.

13. Did you drive too fast when the police stopped your car?

14. I didn't realize you had had to go to court.

15. Their friends are currently sailing around the world in a dinghy.

Lösung 37

1. I was ill this year, but next year I **will work (am working, am going to work)** at my father's company during the school holiday. **3**

2. The architect has been drawing the plans for the new bank since November.

3. After the rabbit had delivered all the Easter eggs, he hopped back to his hole.

4. She **has played** tennis many times so far this summer. **5**

5. I had only read a few pages when I had to stop.

6. When I came home from work yesterday, I turned on the light because it **was** already dark. **4**

7. The cleaning lady swept the floor after she **had polished** the windows. **8**

8. Call the police quickly! The man has been badly hurt in an accident.

9. **Do** you usually **hurry** so much on your way to work? **2**

10. Did you go anywhere after you **had eaten** out at the restaurant? **8**

11. After we **had listened** to his speech for nearly an hour, we left the lecture. **8**

12. After the cow **had been butchered**, the meat was cut, wrapped, and frozen. **8**

13. **Were** you **driving** too fast when the police stopped your car? **7**

14. I didn't realize you had had to go to court.

15. Their friends are currently sailing around the world in a dinghy.

Übung 38

1. The harried businessman visits his psychiatrist every week.

2. After he had written a letter to Uncle Fritz, he wrote one to Aunt Matilda.

3. I left my car at the garage four hours ago; does the mechanic still work on it?

4. We had just returned from the park when our parents arrived.

5. The bank is opening its 100th branch next month.

6. Have you visited the Taj Mahal when you have gone to India last year?

7. By the time the party was over, the fire in the fireplace had already burnt out.

8. You don't need to make tea; I've already done it.

9. I spent an hour looking for my friends.

10. You're overweight because you've been eating too much.

11. The man couldn't buy his wife a pair of gloves for Christmas because he forgot her size.

12. My aunt often spends the summer at the sea and the winter in the city over the past 20 years.

13. The pedestrian was picked up by the ambulance after he was run over by a car.

14. He cooks his own dinners for the last year.

15. Whom did you talk to on the telephone when your boss suddenly entered the room?

Lösung 38

1. The harried businessman visits his psychiatrist every week.

2. After he had written a letter to Uncle Fritz, he wrote one to Aunt Matilda.

3. I left my car at the garage four hours ago; **is** the mechanic still **working** on it? **1**

4. We had just returned from the park when our parents arrived.

5. The bank is opening its 100th branch next month.

6. **Did** you **visit** the Taj Mahal when you **went** to India last year? **4**

7. By the time the party was over, the fire in the fireplace had already burnt out.

8. You don't need to make tea; I've already done it.

9. I spent an hour looking for my friends.

10. You're overweight because you've been eating too much.

11. The man couldn't buy his wife a pair of gloves for Christmas because he **had forgotten** her size. **8**

12. My aunt **has** often **spent** the summer at the sea and the winter in the city over the past 20 years. **5**

13. The pedestrian was picked up by the ambulance after he **had been** run over by a car. **8**

14. He **has been cooking** his own dinners for the last year. **6**

15. Whom **were** you **talking** to on the telephone when your boss suddenly entered the room? **7**

Übung 39

1. How long do you collect stamps?
2. When you called, we were trying to decide whether to invite you to our party or not.
3. He just combed his hair when a gust of wind blew it out of place.
4. We picked up our new car last week; first we must pay for it, then we can drive it away.
5. How long were you in the coffee shop before your wife came?
6. He had written four letters to her before she finally answered.
7. The businessman attends many meetings since he started working for his new company.
8. You can't speak to the boss now. He attends a meeting in Berlin.
9. The waitress removed our plates almost before we'd finished our meal.
10. The boy chews his fingernails since the age of five.
11. How many times do you try to give up smoking so far?
12. After his first child was born, the father celebrated by handing out cigars.
13. We are usually going to bed at 9:00 p. m., but on weekends we are staying up until 10:00 p. m.
14. The teacher cleaned the blackboard before the pupils copied what she wrote on it.
15. What happened after the concert had finished?

Lösung 39

1. How long **have** you **been collecting** stamps? **6**

2. When you called, we were trying to decide whether to invite you to our party or not.

3. He **had** just **combed** his hair when a gust of wind blew it out of place. **8**

4. We picked up our new car last week; first we **had to pay** for it, then we **could drive** it away. **4**

5. How long **had** you **been** in the coffee shop before your wife came? **8**

6. He had written four letters to her before she finally answered.

7. The businessman **has attended** many meetings since he started working for his new company. **5**

8. You can't speak to the boss now. He **is attending** a meeting in Berlin. **1**

9. The waitress removed our plates almost before we'd finished our meal.

10. The boy **has been chewing** his fingernails since the age of five. **6**

11. How many times **have** you **tried** to give up smoking so far? **5**

12. After his first child **had been born**, the father celebrated by handing out cigars. **8**

13. We usually **go** to bed at 9:00 p. m., but on weekends we **stay** up until 10:00 p. m. **2**

14. The teacher **had cleaned** the blackboard before the pupils copied what she **had written** on it. **8**

15. What happened after the concert had finished?

Übung 40

1. We will be able to buy a color television set when we get our Christmas bonus.
2. The sun is usually shining all day in Spain in the summer.
3. After he wrote a book of poems, the author started a novel.
4. As soon as she'd finished school, she started looking for a job.
5. When have you gotten a promotion and a raise in salary?
6. She already had too much coffee today.
7. We got a flat tire as we were crossing the world's longest bridge.
8. The movie star mentioned that she just finished a new movie.
9. I'll bet you're waiting for me for at least an hour, aren't you?
10. Did you unpack your bags immediately after you'd returned from Greece?
11. Are you planning to come to my birthday party next week?
12. The old woman was sick for a year before she died.
13. Just at the moment we drove by the leaning Tower of Pisa, it fell over.
14. How many times have I told you not to forget to turn off the gas?
15. After he looked at his watch, the man hurried off down the street.

Lösung 40

1. We will be able to buy a color television set when we get our Christmas bonus.

2. The sun usually **shines** all day in Spain in the summer. **2**

3. After he **had written** a book of poems, the author started a novel. **8**

4. As soon as she'd finished school, she started looking for a job.

5. When **did** you **get** a promotion and a raise in salary? **4**

6. She **has** already **had** too much coffee today. **5**

7. We got a flat tire as we were crossing the world's longest bridge.

8. The movie star mentioned that she **had** just **finished** a new movie. **8**

9. I'll bet you **have been waiting** for me for at least an hour, **haven't** you? **6**

10. Did you unpack your bags immediately after you'd returned from Greece?

11. Are you planning to come to my birthday party next week?

12. The old woman **had been** sick for a year before she died. **8**

13. Just at the moment we **were driving** by the leaning Tower of Pisa, it fell over. **7**

14. How many times have I told you not to forget to turn off the gas?

15. After he **had looked** at his watch, the man hurried off down the street. **8**

Übung 41

1. We are generally trying to feed our cat at the same time every day.
2. We've enjoyed the scenery very much on our last trip to the States.
3. We haven't seen each other in years, have we?
4. I'm playing table-tennis against the city champion next weekend.
5. Look at that! The car drives the wrong way down a one-way street.
6. The young woman saves her pennies for years to buy her wedding shoes. Now she has enough.
7. It always seems to rain in August, just when we want to go on vacation.
8. The last time we went to church was on Easter Sunday.
9. We've been looking for a new and bigger apartment for several months.
10. We got a notice from the doctor after we already paid our bill.
11. We nearly froze while we were waiting for Aunt Margaret's train to arrive.
12. Our soccer team is currently leading the league.
13. We bet on the horses when we go to the track next week.
14. The insurance company paid the claim after the fire damage had been determined.
15. A tremendous storm hit while we vacationed on Sylt.

Lösung 41

1. We generally **try** to feed our cat at the same time every day. **2**
2. We **enjoyed** the scenery very much on our last trip to the States. **4**
3. We haven't seen each other in years, have we?
4. I'm playing table-tennis against the city champion next weekend.
5. Look at that! The car **is driving** the wrong way down a one-way street. **1**
6. The young woman **has been saving** her pennies for years to buy her wedding shoes. Now she has enough. **6**
7. It always seems to rain in August, just when we want to go on vacation.
8. The last time we went to church was on Easter Sunday.
9. We've been looking for a new and bigger apartment for several months.
10. We got a notice from the doctor after we **had** already **paid** our bill. **8**
11. We nearly froze while we were waiting for Aunt Margaret's train to arrive.
12. Our soccer team is currently leading the league.
13. We **will bet (are betting, are going to bet)** on the horses when we go to the track next week. **3**
14. The insurance company paid the claim after the fire damage had been determined.
15. A tremendous storm hit while we **were vacationing** on Sylt. **7**

Übung 42

1. It says in the newspaper that Clark's department store offers sheets on sale today only.
2. When have you had time to clean the house so thoroughly?
3. How long have you been smoking that brand of cigars?
4. While the secretary typed the letter, her boss suddenly thought of some corrections.
5. After the man had already dropped the letter into the mailbox, he suddenly remembered that there was no stamp on it.
6. It seems like they build our house for a year already.
7. I don't believe you! I think you're telling me a lie!
8. You aren't going to give in to him so quickly, are you?
9. How many times are you in South America in the last five years?
10. John enjoys listening to his favorite records every afternoon when he comes home from school.
11. After she finished shopping, the woman took the bus home.
12. It has been almost a year since I became a pensioner.
13. On Saturdays, they are allowing their children to watch the late movies on TV.
14. When we travel to Alaska next winter, we take along our warmest clothes.
15. When I was eigth years old, I shaved off our cat's whiskers.

Lösung 42

1. It says in the newspaper that Clark's department store **will offer (is offering, is going to offer)** sheets on sale today only. **3**

2. When **did** you **have** time to clean the house so thoroughly? **4**

3. How long have you been smoking that brand of cigars?

4. While the secretary **was typing** the letter, her boss suddenly thought of some corrections. **7**

5. After the man had already dropped the letter into the mailbox, he suddenly remembered that there was no stamp on it.

6. It seems like they **have been building** our house for a year already. **6**

7. I don't believe you! I think you're telling me a lie!

8. You aren't going to give in to him so quickly, are you?

9. How many times **have** you **been** in South America in the last five years? **5**

10. John enjoys listening to his favorite records every afternoon when he comes home from school.

11. After she **had finished** shopping, the woman took the bus home. **8**

12. It has been almost a year since I became a pensioner.

13. On Saturdays, they **allow** their children to watch the late movies on TV. **2**

14. When we travel to Alaska next winter, we **will take (are taking, are going to take)** along our warmest clothes. **3**

15. When I was eigth years old, I shaved off our cat's whiskers.

Übung 43

1. I have a well-trained dog; he always fetches the morning newspaper from my neighbor's porch.

2. What do you look for among my private possessions?

3. What do you do first when your plane reaches New York tomorrow afternoon?

4. The old lady has been living in the same apartment ever since she married fifty years ago.

5. We forgot to pay our electricity bill last month.

6. Where did you go while your husband was fishing last weekend?

7. The swimmer just breaks the world record for the 100-meter butterfly.

8. After we gave up all hope of seeing him again, he turned up unexpectedly after an absence of ten years.

9. Sometimes he's winding his watch in the morning, sometimes in the evening.

10. The pioneer died because he'd been bitten by a rattlesnake.

11. The chicken crossed the road when it was run over by a boy on a bicycle.

12. We won't have to buy a new refrigerator after all; the old one's running again.

13. You've never tried to stand on your head for an hour, have you?

14. The Indian fakir lies on his bed of nails for half an hour and still shows no sign of pain.

15. Did you happen to meet Henry at the station yesterday? He arrived on the same train as you.

Lösung 43

1. I have a well-trained dog; he always fetches the morning newspaper from my neighbor's porch.

2. What **are** you **looking** for among my private possessions? **1**

3. What **will** you **do (are** you **doing, are** you **going to do)** first when your plane reaches New York tomorrow afternoon? **3**

4. The old lady has been living in the same apartment ever since she married fifty years ago.

5. We forgot to pay our electricity bill last month.

6. Where did you go while your husband was fishing last weekend?

7. The swimmer **has** just **broken** the world record for the 100-meter butterfly. **5**

8. After we **had given up** all hope of seeing him again, he turned up unexpectedly after an absence of ten years. **8**

9. Sometimes he **winds** his watch in the mornings, sometimes in the evening. **2**

10. The pioneer died because he'd been bitten by a rattlesnake.

11. The chicken **was crossing** the road when it was run over by a boy on a bicycle. **7**

12. We won't have to buy a new refrigerator after all; the old one's running again.

13. You've never tried to stand on your head for an hour, have you?

14. The Indian fakir **has been lying** on his bed of nails for half an hour and still has shown no sign of pain. **6 + 5**

15. Did you happen to meet Henry at the station yesterday? He arrived on the same train as you.

Übung 44

1. Do you go to John's birthday party next Saturday?
2. Mr. Green has made at least a dozen phone calls so far this morning.
3. While his friends robbed the bank, one robber stood outside.
4. Please don't bother your father at the moment. He's relaxing after a hard day at work.
5. What do you wait for? Do it now!
6. The woman had just finished waxing her kitchen floor when her son walked in with dirty shoes.
7. Will you please bring a loaf of bread with you on your way home tonight, dear?
8. How often are you bringing your wife flowers? Once a week?
9. The seagulls circle the ship for the past half a day, so we must be getting near land.
10. The lady held her poodle's paw while the dog was being shampooed.
11. I've been expecting a call from my mother all morning.
12. After the winter snows melted, the first birds returned from migration.
13. Did you drink a lot of beer when you went to the Oktoberfest?
14. The teacher teaches the same material many times in his many years of service.
15. You never give up trying to cause trouble, do you?

Lösung 44

1. **Will** you **go (are** you **going, are you going to go)** to John's birthday party next Saturday? **3**

2. Mr. Green has made at least a dozen phone calls so far this morning.

3. While his friends **were robbing** the bank, one robber **stood** outside. **7**

4. Please don't bother your father at the moment. He's relaxing after a hard day at work.

5. What **are** you **waiting** for? Do it now! **1**

6. The woman had just finished waxing her kitchen floor when her son walked in with dirty shoes.

7. Will you please bring a loaf of bread with you on your way home tonight, dear?

8. How often **do** you **bring** your wife flowers? Once a week? **2**

9. The seagulls **have been circling** the ship for the past half a day, so we must be getting near land. **6**

10. The lady held her poodle's paw while the dog was being shampooed.

11. I've been expecting a call from my mother all morning.

12. After the winter snows **had melted**, the first birds returned from migration. **8**

13. Did you drink a lot of beer when you went to the Oktoberfest?

14. The teacher **has taught** the same material many times in his many years of service. **5**

15. You never give up trying to cause trouble, do you?

Übung 45

1. By this time next month, we will move into our new apartment.
2. He'll have spent all his money by the time he's paid again.
3. We think at least a thousand customers come to the opening of our new store tomorrow.
4. The artist works on the marble statue every day for weeks.
5. He's always lucky when he plays roulette, isn't he?
6. We visit the exhibition in Berlin last weekend.
7. Will you complete your work by the beginning of August?
8. Don't disturb the zookeeper; he's feeding the lions in their cage at the moment.
9. We've reached the decision to hire more employees at our meeting yesterday.
10. That's her favorite book; she reads it at least four times.
11. Do you presently consider writing a book about your experiences?
12. Up to now, we watch every show of the new television series.
13. John interrupted us while we discussed whether to go to the new Chinese restaurant or not.
14. The thief confessed that he broke into a number of houses.
15. The people in the apartment shout at each other all morning; I wish they would stop.

Lösung 45

1. By this time next month, we **will have moved** into our new apartment. **9**
2. He'll have spent all his money by the time he's paid again.
3. We think at least a thousand customers **will come (are coming, are going to come)** to the opening of our new store tomorrow. **3**
4. The artist **has been working** on the marble statue every day for weeks. **6**
5. He's always lucky when he plays roulette, isn't he?
6. We **visited** the exhibition in Berlin last weekend. **4**
7. **Will** you **have completed** your work by the beginning of August? **9**
8. Don't disturb the zookeeper; he's feeding the lions in their cage at the moment.
9. We **reached** the decision to hire more employees at our meeting yesterday. **4**
10. That's her favorite book; she **has read** it at least four times. **5**
11. **Are** you presently **considering** writing a book about your experiences? **1**
12. Up to now, we **have watched** every show of the new television series. **5**
13. John interrupted us while we **were discussing** whether to go to the new Chinese restaurant or not. **7**
14. The thief confessed that he **had broken** into a number of houses. **8**
15. The people in the apartment **have been shouting** at each other all morning; I wish they would stop. **6**

Übung 46

1. How many times have you tried to climb Mt. Everest?
2. I'm sure he's shaving off his beard when he returns from vacation.
3. After we had seen enough of the old city, we drove on.
4. She'll learn perfect French by the time she comes back from her year of study in France.
5. The Queen is delivering her speech to Parliament every year in the spring.
6. If we don't leave soon, the play will have begun before we arrive.
7. George Washington told his father that he chopped down the cherry tree.
8. We slept when suddenly a loud noise woke us up.
9. The woman tries dozens of perfumes, but she still hasn't found one she likes.
10. You've been speaking for almost an hour. Don't you realize it's a long-distance call?
11. We'll have to have finished our assignment by the next lesson.
12. We all hope he will recover from his illness by Christmas.
13. I've told you yesterday to be more careful!
14. By the time she goes home this afternoon, the secretary will type nearly thirty letters.
15. At the moment, Mary knits a pair of socks for John, who sleeps on the sofa.

Lösung 46

1. How many times have you tried to climb Mt. Everest?

2. I'm sure he's shaving off his beard when he returns from vacation.

3. After we had seen enough of the old city, we drove on.

4. **She'll have learned** perfect French by the time she comes back from her year of study in France. **9**

5. The Queen **delivers** her speech to Parliament every year in the spring. **2**

6. If we don't leave soon, the play will have begun before we arrive.

7. George Washington told his father that he **had chopped** down the cherry tree. **8**

8. We **were sleeping** when suddenly a loud noise woke us up. **7**

9. The woman **has tried** dozens of perfumes, but she still hasn't found one she likes. **5**

10. You've been speaking for almost an hour. Don't you realize it's a long-distance call?

11. We'll have to have finished our assignment by the next lesson.

12. We all hope he **will have recovered** from his illness by Christmas. **9**

13. I **told** you yesterday to be more careful! **4**

14. By the time she goes home this afternon, the secretary **will have typed** nearly thirty letters. **9**

15. At the moment, Mary **is knitting** a pair of socks for John, who **is sleeping** on the sofa. **1**

Übung 47

1. They will surely return home by 7:00 p. m.
2. My wife has been talking on the phone all morning.
3. By the time he finally gets his degree, he will study for six years.
4. I'm taking the bus every time I go to Berlin.
5. By the year 2000, rockets will have replaced jet planes.
6. Over a hundredt housand replies to the contest arrived by the time it ended last week.
7. While we were looking for the lost watch in the living room and John was searching in the kitchen, Joe was finding it in the bedroom.
8. By the time you see him again, he will get a haircut.
9. How many times have you had to replace the needle on your stereo?
10. You'll certainly have recovered from the shock of winning in the lottery by the time your prize is delivered, won't you?
11. Have you seen the Kremlin when you've been in Moscow?
12. The man recovers very well from his operation, but he is still in pain.
13. The street won't have been repaired by next winter.
14. We arrived in Paris last Tuesday and are here a week already.
15. I hope you'll have gone to the doctor by the next time we see each other.

Lösung 47

1. They **will** surely **have returned** home by 7:00 p. m. **9**

2. My wife has been talking on the phone all morning.

3. By the time he finally gets his degree, he **will have been studying** for six years. **9**

4. I **take** the bus every time I go to Berlin. **2**

5. By the year 2000, rockets will have replaced jet planes.

6. Over a hundred thousand replies to the contest **had arrived** by the time it ended last week. **8**

7. While we were looking for the lost watch in the living room and John was searching in the kitchen, Joe **found** it in the bedroom. **4**

8. By the time you see him again, he **will have got** a haircut. **9**

9. How many times have you had to replace the needle on your stereo?

10. You'll certainly have recovered from the shock of winning in the lottery by the time your prize is delivered, won't you?

11. **Did** you **see** the Kremlin when you **were** in Moscow? **4**

12. The man **is recovering** very well from his operation, but he is still in pain. **1**

13. The street won't have been repaired by next winter.

14. We arrived in Paris last Tuesday and **have been** here a week already. **5**

15. I hope you'll have gone to the doctor by the next time we see each other.

Übung 48

1. In the newspaper, it says the new city hall will have been completed by next autumn.
2. After he looked for hours, he finally found his mistake.
3. The baby sleeps for more than ten hours already.
4. Did you have to get a new washing machine when your old one broke down, or could it be fixed?
5. The maid has been working for the Smiths for a quarter of a century.
6. We are sometimes celebrating Christmas in the Bahamas, but more often we are spending our holiday at home.
7. Hurry, and you'll finish your homework before your music lesson begins.
8. Please call her soon, or otherwise she will have already left.
9. The child now tries to repair the expensive vase which he broke while playing football in the house.
10. Do you think you'll finish painting the living-room by the time mother arrives?
11. Have you been able to reach your wife yet to tell her the good news about your promotion?
12. He met a new girlfriend while he waited for his old one to come.
13. By this time next year, the couple will celebrate their Golden Anniversary, and the man his 80th birthday.
14. I'm not going to sell my car until it's at least five years old.
15. She'll have taken care of the laundry by Saturday at the latest.

Lösung 48

1. In the newspaper, it says the new city hall will have been completed by next autumn.
2. After he **had looked** for hours, he finally found his mistake. **8**
3. The baby **has been sleeping** for more than ten hours already. **6**
4. Did you have to get a new washing machine when your old one broke down, or could it be fixed?
5. The maid has been working for the Smiths for a quarter of a century.
6. We sometimes **celebrate** Christmas in the Bahamas, but more often we **spend** our holiday at home. **2**
7. Hurry, and **you'll have finished** your homework before your music lesson begins. **9**
8. Please call her soon, or otherwise she will have already left.
9. The child **is** now **trying** to repair the expensive vase which he broke while playing football in the house. **1**
10. Do you think **you'll have finished** painting the living-room by the time mother arrives? **9**
11. Have you been able to reach your wife yet to tell her the good news about your promotion?
12. He met a new girlfriend while he **was waiting** for his old one to come. **7**
13. By this time next year, the couple **will have celebrated** their Golden Anniversary, and the man his 80th birthday. **9**
14. I'm not going to sell my car until it's at least five years old.
15. She'll have taken care of the laundry by Saturday at the latest.

Übung 49

1. I'll read the famous author's latest book by the time I meet him.
2. How long do you have your dog?
3. I travel around the world next summer. Do you want to join me?
4. I can hardly believe it. The sun finally shines again after so many rainy days.
5. Mother still baked cookies when the children came home from school.
6. By what date do you think you will move to England?
7. Aren't we ever going to reach our hotel? I feel like I carry these suitcases for ten miles.
8. Every time the man visits his girlfriend, he's taking a box of candy with him.
9. The excited parents informed the police that their child was kidnapped.
10. My neighbor isn't home. He's studying the plant life on Easter Island.
11. The Queen is flying to Australia next month to greet her subjects.
12. I'll have answered your letter by next Friday at the latest.
13. The telephone repairman has quickly repaired my telephone the last time I called him.
14. My car will have to have had a thorough overhaul by the time I go to the next inspection.
15. On Friday, he'll have his Rolls-Royce for exactly two years.

Lösung 49

1. **I'll have read** the famous author's latest book by the time I meet him. **9**

2. How long **have** you **had** your dog? **5**

3. I **will travel (am travelling, am going to travel)** around the world next summer. Do you want to join me? **3**

4. I can hardly believe it. The sun **is** finally **shining** again after so many rainy days. **1**

5. Mother **was** still **baking** cookies when the children came home from school. **7**

6. By what date do you think you **will have moved** to England? **9**

7. Aren't we ever going to reach our hotel? I feel like I **have been carrying** these suitcases for ten miles. **6**

8. Every time the man visits his girlfriend, he **takes** a box of candy with him. **2**

9. The excited parents informed the police that their child **had been kidnapped. 8**

10. My neighbor isn't home. He's studying the plant life on Easter Island.

11. The Queen is flying to Australia next month to greet her subjects.

12. I'll have answered your letter by next Friday at the latest.

13. The telephone repairman quickly **repaired** my telephone the last time I called him. **4**

14. My car will have to have had a thorough overhaul by the time I go to the next inspection.

15. On Friday, **he'll have had** his Rolls-Royce for exactly two years. **9**

Übung 50

1. How many times do you try to rob a bank so far?
2. When the man was interviewed, he said he was asked the same questions the day before.
3. By the time you finish your job, I will have finished mine, too.
4. How long have you been painting for a living?
5. All the trees in this forest will be cut down and sawed into lumber by 1985.
6. You haven't ever tasted my mother's old-fashioned custard pie, have you?
7. Last year, his company has sold a million dollars worth of equipment.
8. While we were looking for a new apartment, we found exactly what we wanted.
9. When is the furniture store finally going to deliver the other chair you ordered?
10. A merger is being planned between the two conglomerates.
11. By the time he's 70, he'll be retired for five years.
12. I'm never getting used to winter until it's nearly over.
13. You'll certainly have finished composing your masterpiece by next summer, won't you?
14. Every day, he reads his newspaper on the train on his way home from work.
15. At the moment the postman rang the doorbell, I sat in the bathtub.

Lösung 50

1. How many times **have** you **tried** to rob a bank so far? **5**
2. When the man was interviewed, he said he **had been asked** the same questions the day before. **8**
3. By the time you finish your job, I will have finished mine, too.
4. How long have you been painting for a living?
5. All the trees in this forest **will have been cut** down and sawed into lumber by 1985. **9**
6. You haven't ever tasted my mother's old-fashioned custard pie, have you?
7. Last year, his company **sold** a million dollars worth of equipment. **4**
8. While we were looking for a new apartment, we found exactly what we wanted.
9. When is the furniture store finally going to deliver the other chair you ordered?
10. A merger is being planned between the two conglomerates.
11. By the time he's 70, **he'll have been retired** for five years. **9**
12. I never **get** used to winter until it's nearly over. **2**
13. You'll certainly have finished composing your masterpiece by next summer, won't you?
14. Every day, he reads his newspaper on the train on his way home from work.
15. At the moment the postman rang the doorbell, I **was sitting** in the bathtub. **7**

Grammatikalische Erläuterungen

1: Continuous Present

drückt etwas aus, was in diesem Augenblick geschieht.
Beispiel: I am eating cookies now.
Engländer lassen meistens das Wort «now» weg, da das Continuous Present bereits das «jetzt» einschließt. Ist der Satz grammatikalisch richtig, ist das Wort «now» überflüssig. Ist der Satz grammatikalisch verkehrt, wird er durch Hinzufügung des Wortes now nicht richtig.

Das Continuous Present wird gebildet aus der entsprechenden Form des Hilfverbs to be und der Stammform des Verbs + ing-Endung.
Beispiel: I am drinking a beer at the moment.
He is drinking a beer at the moment.
We are drinking a beer at the moment.

2: Simple Present

drückt ein Geschehen aus, das mit Regelmäßigkeit vorkommt oder mit Regelmäßigkeit nicht vorkommt.
Beispiel: I eat every workday. I never eat on a Sunday. I fast.
Ein regelmäßiges Vorkommen wird ausgedrückt durch Wörter wie: often, seldom, sometimes, always, never.
Beispiel: I sometimes (often, seldom, always, never) come home late.

Es drückt auch Tatsachen aus.
Beispiel: I like apples.
Manchmal drückt der Satz sowohl ein regelmäßiges Vorkommen wie auch Tatsachen aus.
Beispiel: The Queen smokes Marlboro cigarettes.

Das Simple Present ist in der Regel die gleiche Form wie die Grundform eines Verbs, nur in der 3. Person Singular fügt man in der Regel eine «s»- oder «es»-Endung hinzu.
Beispiel: I read a newspaper every day.
He reads a newspaper every day.
I watch television every evening.
He watches television every evening.

3: Future

Wie es üblicherweise in einfachsten Formen verstanden wird, das heißt als ein zukünftiges Ereignis, wird das Future hauptsächlich auf drei Weisen dargestellt:

1. Auf die bekannte Weise mit «will» oder «shall».
Beispiel: I will (shall) see him tomorrow.
2. In Form des Continuous Present.
Beispiel: I am seeing him tomorrow.
3. Auf idiomatische Weise.
Beispiel: I am going to see him tomorrow.
(Wir werden später noch auf eine weitere Future tense zu sprechen kommen.)

Zur will/shall-Weise:
Sie trägt offiziell den Namen Simple Future, wird am häufigsten für formelles Sprechen und formelle Korrespondenz verwendet und wird wie folgt konjugiert: Wenn man normal spricht, lautet die erste Person Singular und Plural «shall» und alle anderen Personen Singular und Plural «will».

	Singular	Plural
1. Person	I shall	we shall
2. Person	you will	you will
3. Person	he, she, it will	they will

Will man betonen, daß die Sache wirklich passieren wird, dann ist es genau umgekehrt. Wo im normalen Gespräch ein «will» steht, steht nun ein «shall», wo normalerweise ein «shall» steht, steht nun ein «will». Soviel zur offiziellen Version.

Was die Praxis anbetrifft, gibt es den nicht zu leugnenden Trend, für alle Personen Singular und Plural einfach «will» zu sagen. Dies stammt vielleicht daher, daß nie ganz zu erkennen oder zu beweisen ist, ob eine Betonung gemeint ist, und weil im gesprochenen Englisch meistens auf «I'll» verkürzt wird und daraus nicht zu erkennen ist, ob «I will» oder «I shall» gemeint ist.

Zur Continuous Present-Weise:
Diese uns bereits als Continuous Present bekannte Form, die Zukunft auszudrücken, stellt nur die Zukunft dar, wenn ein Wort, das die Zukunft ausdrückt, im Satz vorhanden ist oder dies aus dem vorausgehenden Satzinhalt unmißverständlich hervorgeht.

Beispiel: I am flying to Frankfurt tomorrow.
oder
Where are you going at the weekend?
I am going home.
(«at the weekend» muß nicht wiederholt werden.)

Diese Form drückt oft eine bereits geplante Tätigkeit aus.

Zur idiomatischen Weise:
Ein Idiom (eine idiomatische Redewendung) ist ein Wort oder sind Wörter, die nicht wörtlich zu verstehen sind.

Beispiel: to pull someone's leg. Aus den Wörtern selbst geht nicht hervor, was die Bedeutung sein soll. Man muß einfach wissen, daß der Satz «jemanden auf den Arm nehmen» heißt – eine Redewendung, die bei einer wörtlichen Übersetzung ins Englische ebenfalls nicht zu verstehen wäre.

«I am going to see you tomorrow» stellt die idiomatische Zukunft dar, weil von gehen gar keine Rede ist. «I am going to» heißt nichts anderes als «ich werde», und wenn man dem Sein-Verb in Verbindung mit «going to» und einem darauffolgenden Verb begegnet, handelt es sich um die Zukunft.

Beispiel: I am going to see ...
I am going to write ...
I am going to go ...

Auf diese Form der Zukunft ist besonders zu achten, weil sie, obwohl komplizierter als die anderen Formen, die weitaus gängigste im Umgangsenglisch ist.

4: Simple Past

drückt eine abgeschlossene Zeit in der Vergangenheit aus, egal wie weit sie zurückliegt. Sie ist die am meisten verwendete Zeit in der Vergangenheit. Sie wird charakterisiert durch Wörter wie «yesterday, last week, last month, last year».
Beispiel: I saw him yesterday.

Ein regelmäßiges Verb im Simple Past wird gebildet durch Anhängung einer «d»- oder «ed»-Endung.
Beispiel: I work ten hours every day.
I worked ten hours yesterday.

Ein unregelmäßiges Verb im Simple Past wird entweder gebildet durch völlige Veränderung der Form
Beispiel: I go home every night.
I went home last night.

oder es ändert sich überhaupt nicht.
Beispiel: I cut myself while shaving every morning.
I cut myself while shaving yesterday morning.

Das einzige, was alle unregelmäßigen Verben gemeinsam miteinander haben, ist also die Tatsache, daß sie *keine* «d»- oder «ed»-Endung in der Vergangenheit erhalten.

5: Present Perfect

drückt entweder eine unabgeschlossene Zeit in der Gegenwart oder eine unbenannte Zeit in der Vergangenheit aus. Drückt es eine unabgeschlossene Zeit in der Gegenwart aus (das heißt eine Zeit, die zwar in der Vergangenheit begann, die jedoch noch läuft), wird diese charakterisiert in Verbindung mit Zeitangaben wie «today, this week, this month, this year, this morning (wenn es noch heute morgen ist)» verwendet. Andere Schlüsselwörter für das Present Perfect sind «since, for, just, already, yet, still, because, ever, how many? und how often?»

Beispiel: I have been here since 8 a. m.
I have been here for four hours.

Drückt das Present Perfect eine unbenannte Zeit in der Vergangenheit aus, erfüllt es in der Regel eine von zwei Aufgaben: Entweder drückt sie Tatsachen aus

Beispiel: I have done my homework.

oder sie stellt eine Frage für eine Ja- oder Nein-Antwort und gibt die dazugehörende Antwort.

Beispiel: Have you done your homework? Yes, I have.

Das Present Perfect ist die schwierigste Zeit für Deutsche. Das hat zwei Ursachen:

1. Es gibt diese Zeit in der deutschen Sprache nicht.
2. Der Wortlaut dieser Zeit ist zum Verwechseln ähnlich mit der Zeit, in der der Deutsche häufig die Vergangenheit ausdrückt. Das führt zu unmöglichen Übersetzungen, wie beispielsweise der folgenden: «Ich habe meine Mutter gestern gesehen.» – «I have seen my mother yesterday.» Dieser Satz ist deswegen im Englischen unmöglich, weil man niemals «I have seen» mit «yesterday» in Verbindung bringen darf, denn «yesterday» drückt eine abgeschlossene Zeit in der Vergangenheit aus, während «I have seen» eine unabgeschlossene Zeit in der Gegenwart oder eine unbenannte Zeit in der Vergangenheit ausdrückt.

Das Present Perfect wird gebildet aus der entsprechenden Form des Hilfsverbs to have und dem Past Participle (der sogenannten dritten Form des Verbs).

Beispiel: I have gone to New York many times.
He has gone to New York many times.

6: Present Perfect Continuous

Diese Zeit fügt dem Present Perfect ein weiteres Element hinzu, indem sie eine sich wiederholende Tätigkeit oder einen Bewegungsablauf entweder direkt oder indirekt ausdrückt. Sie kann in der Regel auch dort eingesetzt werden, wo das Present Perfect angewendet wird.
Beispiel: I have been trying to reach you all day.
Es ist die mehr oder weniger direkt ausgedrückte Idee:
«I have been trying again and again and again.»
Beispiel: I have been waiting for you for two hours!
Dieses Beispiel ist noch subtiler. Auch hier handelt es sich nicht einfach um eine noch andauernde Tätigkeit, sondern um eine Wiederholung, die nicht direkt ausgedrückt wird. Der Sinn: «I have been waiting and waiting and waiting ...»

Das Present Perfect Continuous wird gebildet aus einer entsprechenden Form des Hilfsverbs to have + been und der Grundform des Verbs mit einer ing-Endung.
Beispiel: I have been watching television for twenty minutes.
Achten Sie auf Schlüsselwörter Wie «since, for, just, already und how long?»

7: Past Continuous

Das Past Continuous wird auf zwei Weisen verwendet:
1. Diese Zeit wird verwendet, um eine fortlaufende Tätigkeit in der Vergangenheit darzustellen, die durch irgendein Ereignis in der Vergangenheit unterbrochen wird. Die laufende Tätigkeit wird durch das Past Continuous, die Unterbrechung durch das Simple Past ausgedrückt.
Beispiel: I was walking down the street when I heard the crash.
Achten Sie auf Schlüsselwörter, wie zum Beispiel «when» oder «while».

2. Diese Zeit wird verwendet, um zwei gleichzeitig laufende Tätigkeiten in der Vergangenheit darzustellen.
Beispiel: While John was bathing, his wife was making breakfast.
Achten Sie auf das Schlüsselwort «while».

Wie man aus den obigen Erklärungen und Beispielen erkennen kann, kommt das Past Continuous nie als alleinstehendes Verb in einem Satz vor, es sei denn, daß die zweite fehlende Zeit vorausgesetzt, aber nicht ausgesprochen wird.
Beispiel: Die Antwort auf die Frage «What were you doing when I called you yesterday?» kann lauten: «I was bathing.» Der fehlende Satzteil «... when you called me yesterday» braucht nicht wiederholt zu werden, er wird vorausgesetzt.

Es muß darauf hingewiesen werden, daß zwei fortlaufende Tätigkeiten, die zur selben Zeit in der Vergangenheit ausgeübt werden, nicht notwendigerweise durch das Past Continuous ausgedrückt werden müssen. Soll es sich um die Darstellung von Fakten oder von regelmäßig vorkommenden Ereignissen handeln, verwendet man das Simple Past.
Beispiel: Because they were in a hurry to catch their train, he packed their bags while she cleaned the house.

Das letzte Beispiel wird in diesem Buch nicht behandelt, da es keine Probleme für Deutsche darstellt.
Das Past Continuous wird gebildet aus dem Hilfsverb to be in Simple Past und der Stammform des Verbs + ing-Endung.

8: Past Perfect

Das Past Perfect darf nur verwendet werden, wenn es zwei Verben im Satz gibt, die in einer zeitlichen Sequenz in der Vergangenheit zueinander stehen. Auf gut deutsch: Die zwei Verben drücken Ereignisse in der Vergangenheit aus, von denen ein Ereignis weiter in der Vergangenheit zurückliegt als das andere. Aus diesem Grund erscheinen in einem Satz, welcher korrekt das Past Perfect anwendet, oft die Schlüsselwörter «before» and «after». In so einem Satz wird das weiter in der Vergangenheit liegende Ereignis durch das Past Perfect und das nicht so weit in der Vergangenheit liegende Ereignis durch das Simple Past ausgedrückt.
Beispiel: Before the little boy went to the zoo he had never seen a camel. After he had seen a camel he dreamt about it.

Anders ausgedrückt: Enthält ein Satz nur ein einziges Verb oder aber zwei Verben, die nicht Ereignisse darstellen, die in zeitlicher Sequenz in der Vergangenheit zueinander stehen, darf das Past Perfect nicht verwendet werden. Der typische deutsche Irrtum ist, das Past Perfect für eine abgeschlossene Handlung, die weit in der Vergangenheit liegt, zu verwenden. Wie weit zurück ein Ereignis in der Vergangenheit liegt, spielt keine Rolle. Ist das Ereignis abgeschlossen und steht es allein im Satz, muß das Simple Past und nicht das Past Perfect verwendet werden.

Das Past Perfect wird gebildet aus dem Hilfsverb to have in Simple Past in Verbindung mit dem Past Participle (der sogenannten dritten Form des Verbs).
Beispiel: After he had eaten, he went to bed.

9: Future Perfect und Future Perfect Continuous

Das Future Perfect bezieht sich auf eine Zeit in der Zukunft, zu der ein Vorgang abgeschlossen sein wird.
Beispiel: Next Tuesday John will have worked for the company for ten years.

Häufig wird die Präposition «by» verwendet, um der Zeit die Bedeutung von «bis spätestens» zu verleihen.
Beispiel: By this time next week, we will have solved the problem.

Das Future Perfect Continuous hat eine andere Aussagekraft. Es drückt in erster Linie nicht eine Tatsache aus, sondern bringt entweder die sich wiederholende Handlung oder die für die Handlung benötigte Zeitspanne zum Ausdruck, die zu einem Ergebnis in der Zukunft führt.
Beispiel: Next Tuesday John will have been working for the company for ten years.

Dieser Satz kann so oder so gemeint sein, entweder «year after year for ten long years! That's a damn long time!» oder aber auch «Next Tuesday John will have been working for the company for ten years and in all of those years he was not out sick for one day. That's an accomplishment to be proud of!»

Wie der Satz auch gemeint ist, sei dahingestellt. Er drückt auf jeden Fall kein bloßes Statement, keine gefühlsneutrale Aussage aus, wie es beim Future Perfect der Fall ist.

Das Future Perfect wird gebildet aus will oder shall + have + Present Participle (der sogenannten dritten Form des Verbs).
Beispiel: We shall have finished our work by this time tomorrow.

Das Future Perfect Continuous wird gebildet aus will oder shall + have (has) been + der Stammform des Verbs + ing-Endung.
Beispiel: We shall have been working for five days by Saturday afternoon.

Englisch

Uwe Kreisel / Pamela Ann Tabbert
Multilingua Englisch *von Anfang an*
(Buch: rororo 60481 / Buch mit Audio-CD: rororo 60435 / Toncassette: rororo 60482)

English Two *Englisch reden und verstehen. Ein Aufbaukurs*
(Buch: rororo 19320, Toncassette: 19321)

Ultimate Idioms *Der Schlüssel zu den britischen und amerikanischen Redewendungen*
(rororo 18492)

American Slang in letzter Minute *Ein Sprachführer für Kurzentschlossene*
(Buch: rororo 19623 / Buch mit Toncassette: rororo 19624 / Toncassette: rororo 19705)

Lust and Love *English for Flirts. Ein Sprachkurs zum Annähern*
(rororo 19976)

Paul Krieger
Supertrain Grammar *Der direkte Weg zu englischer Grammatik*
(rororo 60107)

Emer O'Sullivan / Dietmar Rösler
Modern Talking *Englisches Quasselbuch mit Sprüchen und Widersprüchen*
(rororo 18427)

rororo sprachen

Ernest Pasakarnis
Master your Idioms *Der Schlüssel zu den englischen Redewendungen*
(rororo 18491)

Christa von Staden
See you later, alligator! *Sprachgewandt mit animalischen Idioms*
(rororo 60367)

Ein Gesamtverzeichnis aller lieferbaren Titel der Reihe *rororo sprachen* finden Sie in der *Rowohlt Revue*. Vierteljährlich neu. Kostenlos in Ihrer Buchhandlung.

Rowohlt im Internet: www.rowohlt.de

3668/1